# HOW TO DESIGN EFFECTIVE STORE ADVERTISING

# M. L. ROSENBLUM

HOW TO DESIGN EFFECTIVE STORE ADVERTISING

# INTRODUCTION

I've been in Retail Advertising for a few decades. I've been teaching a class at the New York University School of Retailing for a quarter-century. In these years I've sought after facile methods to train young people in our crafts. We've fumbled with big charts, with blackboard demonstrations, with slides. Miraculously some of the people turned out well — they progressed mainly because of their own aptitudes.

Now "Rosy's" book arrives on the Retail Scene. I believe that our long crusade is over. This book is so sensible, so easy to grasp, so full of fundamental instruction that I predict it will be a great boon to those who labor in the retail vineyards.

Only "Rosy" could have written this book. He has not only been through the mill — his advertising at Macy's, Bamberger's and A&S has been admired and copied from coast to coast — but he has a way of imparting information which remains in the mind of expert and neophyte alike.

I relish the coincidence of the publishing of this 208-page gem with my tenure as Chairman of the Sales Promotion Division of the National Retail Merchants Association.

*Harold R. Merahn*

Harold H. Merahn
*Vice President,*
*Gertz Long Island*
*Member of Allied Stores Corp.*

*1961*

*Consulting Editor / Judy Young Ocko*

*Typography / Sidney A. Siegel, Master Typo Co., Inc.*

*To my wife Lucille*
*Sales Promotion Director of my life*
*and*
*to all other inspiring*
*Sales Promotion Directors with*
*whom I have worked... especially*
*Dorothy Swenson, the late Richard Weil, Jr.,*
*George Slockbower, Frances Corey and*
*John A. Blum.*

# THANK YOU

To the many people who have helped this book come to be...my thanks.

Thank you to John A. Blum (Sales Promotion Director, Macy's New York) and Charles Vercelli (Business Manager-Sales Promotion, Macy's New York) who have read and listened and argued and suggested. Thank you to the Corporate Executives of Macy's and Arthur L. Manchee, President of Macy's New York, who, over the years, have encouraged me to experiment and have given me the freedom that is the climate of creativity. I have tried to use it to their profit...and not at their expense. And to all the other people who have helped... knowingly and unknowingly, my deepest thanks and appreciation.

Clara Apfel
Stephen Baker
Harold Balian
Dick Basile
William Berta
Robert A. Bowerman
Ruth Branigan
Marilou Capstaff
Lewis Chapin
Jules Chayt
Dorothy Chinitz
Robert Cinquino
Edmund Cluett
Julia Coburn
Kenneth Collins
Myrthine Corley
John L. Coughlin
Tom Counahan
George R. Cruze, Jr.
Randolph D'Amico
Nat Davidoff
Charles Davis
Peter DeNapoli
Charles Derosier
Jane D'Esposito
Roy Doty
Joe Durst
Charles Edwards
Walter Einsel
Edward Engle
Rita Farrell
Hildegarde Fisher
George Freedman
William M. Freeman
Sylvio Galterio
Steve Gavin
Robert Geiger
Ruby Goldstein
Monroe Green
Herbert Greenwald
Abe Greiss
Tom Grey
Mildred Harris
Ralph Heineman
Mino Hiromuro
Arthur Hirschhorn
Dorothy Hood
Fred Hoyt
Aristedes Kambanis
Max Kastenbaum
Suzanne Kaye
Irving Kleinfeld
Meyer Kling
Joseph Kovacs
Richard Alan Leahy
John Less
Manfred Lomnitz
Ira Low
Bob Martin*
Charles Marshall
Veronica Marshall
Lottie Martinengo

Elizabeth McCauley
Harold R. Merahn
Elizabeth Mirijanian
Catherine Morabito
Eric Mulvany
Shirley Murray
Robert Pace
Dominic Picini
Alvin Pimsler
B. Lewis Posen
Leo Rackow
Andrew Ragona
Kenneth Richards
Harry Rodman
Peter Rosenblum
Stephen Rosenblum
John Rosmini
Gennaro Ruggiero
Harold Schapps
J. Nieder-Schabbehard
Harold Schoemer
Arthur See
Warren Sefton
M. Seklemian
Dorothy Shock
William Simon
Andrew Szoerke
Louis Tannenbaum
Edward Turano
Percy Varian
Max Walter
Kenneth Walters
Saul White
Carl Wilson
Robert Wilvers


Abraham & Straus
B. Altman & Co.
Arnold Constable
Bamberger's New Jersey
Best & Co.
Bloomingdale's
Bonwit Teller
Famous-Barr
Finchley
Franklin Simon
Galeries Lafayette
Gertz Long Island
Gimbel's
Hahne & Co.
Higbee's
Hochschild, Kohn & Co.
Jordan Marsh
Kaufmann's
Lambert Brothers
Lit Brothers
Lord & Taylor
Macy's New York
Marshall Field & Co.
Meier & Frank
Neiman-Marcus

Nordiska Companiet
Rich's
Robinson's
Rogers Peet & Co.
Saks Fifth Avenue
Saks 34th Street
Sloane's
Spiegel, Inc.
Stern's
Tiffany & Co.
John Wanamaker
Whitehouse & Hardy

The Burlington Free Press
The Chicago Sun-Times
The Chicago Tribune
The Cleveland Press
Hartford Courant
Lafayette Journal & Courier
Long Island Press
Macy Westchester Newspapers
Manchester Evening Herald
Minnesota Herald
Newark Evening News
Newark Star-Ledger
New York Daily Mirror
New York Daily News
New York Herald Tribune
New York Journal Americaan
New York Post
New York Times
New York World-Telegram
The Daily Oklahoman, Oklahoma City Times
Plainfield Courier News
The Providence Evening Bulletin & Journal
The Wall Street Journal
The Washington Post and Times Herald
The Waukegan News-Sun
This Week Magazine
Women's Wear Daily

Newspaper Advertising Executive Association
Retail Advertising Week
Retail Reporting Bureau
School of Retailing, New York University
Tobé-Coburn School for Fashion Careers

Bee Photo
Bettman Archives
Copy Lab Co., Inc.
Ralph Heineman Ad-Aid Service
Jay-See Display
Master Typo Co., Inc.
McGraw-Hill Book Company, Inc.
Photo-Lettering, Inc.
Prentice Hall Inc.
Simon & Schuster

*Art Material from*
*Glasner Art Supply Co. Inc., N.Y.*

# CONTENTS

# IT STARTS WITH THE MERCHANDISE

## 1

A representative of the advertising department, a buyer and an assistant buyer discuss the ad and review the merchandise.

# PRODUCTION OF A NEWSPAPER AD

## "IT STARTS WITH THE MERCHANDISE"

### SALESMEN IN PRINT...

Judy Young Ocko, a gifted advertising writer starts her lectures on retail advertising at the Tobé Coburn School of Fashion Careers with this admonition, "You're a salesman in print. Your tools are newspaper space, printed words and pictures. Your ad must speak for itself, you can't go along with it to explain what you mean. You're like a salesman on the road or behind a counter. You must show your goods to its best advantage and sell its benefits to your customers". Then, and only then does she discuss the mechanics and creativity of advertising writing.

### COME IN, SEE, TOUCH, TRY ON...

Mildred Harris, an astute advertising executive concluded one of her Paris Line-for-Line fashion ads with an invitation that women could not, and did not, turn down. After dramatizing the significant details of the new Paris fashions she wrote, "Tomorrow at 9:45, you must come in, see, touch, try on one of the new Paris Line-for-Line copies". Miss Harris knows merchandise and knows too, that women (customers) react affirmatively to interesting merchandise facts.

### LET'S LOOK AT THE GOODS...

Abe Greiss, assistant creative director of Macy's New York advertising department, who works with more than 50 creative people, is constantly suggesting to his staff when he reviews an ad that seems to be getting nowhere..."Let's take a look at the goods". And they do, whether it's in the Merchandise Loan Room or on the floor. Then they discuss the ad further. For Mr. Greiss too, knows that creativity in advertising is not an abstraction but a reality, and that the best creative solutions to an ad start with the merchandise.

### PORTAL TO PORTAL...

On these two pages and the eight that follow, are forty-one steps in the production of a newspaper ad. The techniques may vary from store to store, but these forty-one steps represent the highlights of the entire complex process. There are many intermediate steps not shown, and variations of the process that depend on the material the store sends to the newspaper. However, no matter what or how, one fact is constant: the ad starts with merchandise, and ends with the merchandise...in the customer's home.

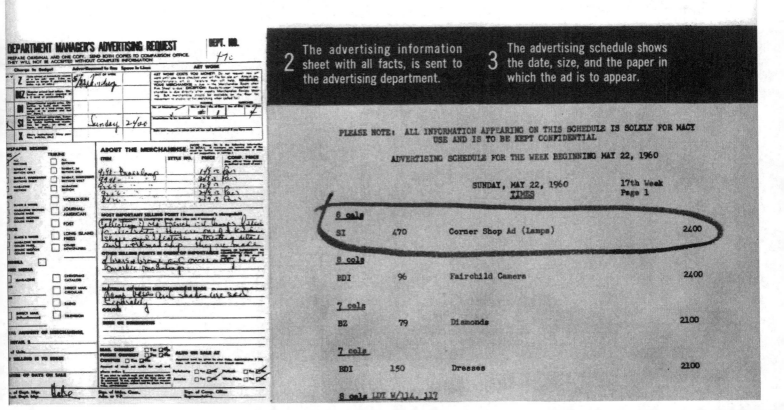

2 The advertising information sheet with all facts, is sent to the advertising department.

3 The advertising schedule shows the date, size, and the paper in which the ad is to appear.

PLEASE NOTE: ALL INFORMATION APPEARING ON THIS SCHEDULE IS SOLELY FOR MACY USE AND IS TO BE KEPT CONFIDENTIAL

ADVERTISING SCHEDULE FOR THE WEEK BEGINNING MAY 22, 1960

SUNDAY, MAY 22, 1960          17th Week
TIMES                         Page 1

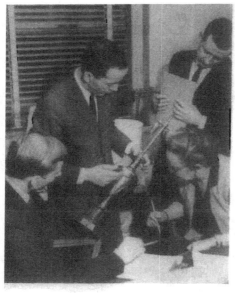

4 The buyer, ad manager, art director and copy writer discuss strategy and points of emphasis.

5 Art Director prepares small layout "roughs" for discussion with ad manager and writer.

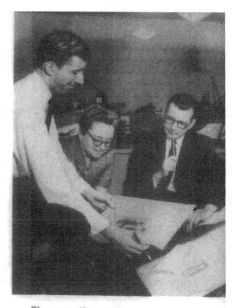

6 The creative group reaches a decision and selects one of the small scale layout "roughs".

7 The copy writer, with the layout rough and the buyer's information sheet, writes the final copy.

8 The art director, with the completed copy, enlarges the small rough to an actual size layout.

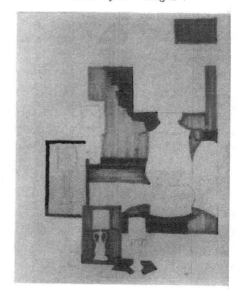

9 The first completed layout stage: the art and the store signature are drawn in boldly.

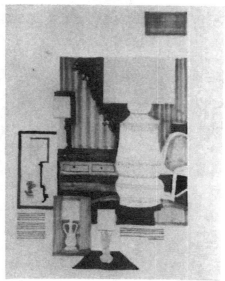

10 The 2nd layout stage: more detail drawn, copy blocks indicated.

11 The 3rd layout stage: all copy and final touches added.

12 The completed layout: all art and copy in proper relationship.

**13** The completed layout is reviewed and approved by the ad manager and is put into production.

**14** Copies of the layout are distributed to everyone concerned with production of the ad.

**15** The photograph is taken to fit space indicated on the layout. (Detail of photo shown below.)

16 Art, step 1: the artist studies the merchandise, traces the position of the art in the layout.

17 Art, step 2: the artist, drawing from the merchandise, completes the rough on tissue.

18 Art, step 3: the rough drawing on tissue is transferred by tracing to drawing paper.

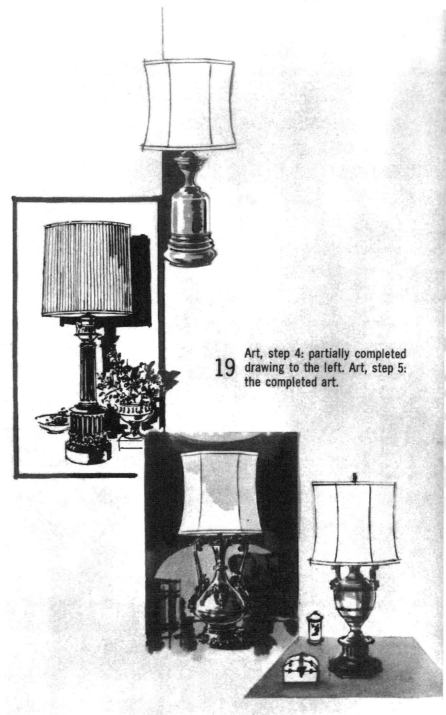

19 Art, step 4: partially completed drawing to the left. Art, step 5: the completed art.

20 Retouching, step 1: the photograph, enlarged to match layout mounted on heavy drawing board.

21 Retouching, step 2: a paper mask frames the section of the photo to be reproduced. The artwork is then cut out and placed over the photograph in the position indicated on the layout.

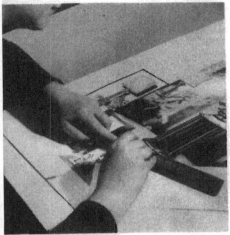

22 Retouching, step 3: flaws are removed with brush and paint.

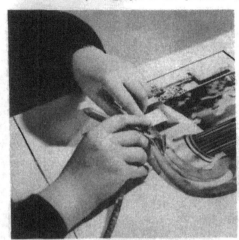

23 Retouching, step 4: the airbrush improves photo tonal values.

24 The artwork OK'd by art director and buyer, is ready for engraver.

25 Production department indicates type, sizes the art and sends all material to the newspaper.

7

26 Engraving, step 1: artwork is photographed to size indicated on layout and marked on art.

27 Engraving, step 2: the exposed film is placed over a light box, all imperfections corrected.

28 Engraving, step 3: the film is exposed to light sensitive metal, then etched in acid solutions.

29 Engraving, step 4: the etched plate is inspected, imperfections and dead metal removed.

30 Engraving, step 5: proof is pulled of the plate, then compared with the original art.

31 A linotype operator sets the body type from the copywriter's original manuscript.

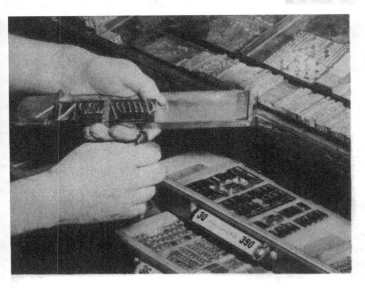

**32** A typographer sets the display (large) type by hand, as indicated on the layout.

**33** Type and plate are put in a form, to follow layout. The ad is now ready to be proved.

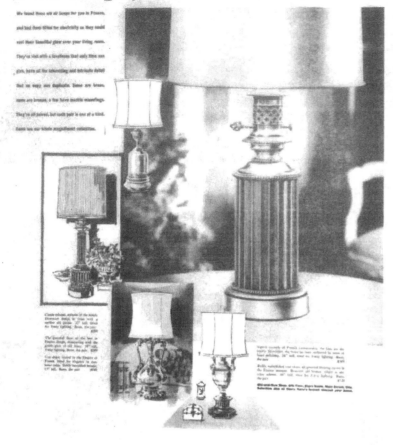

*New lamps from old: a beautiful story*

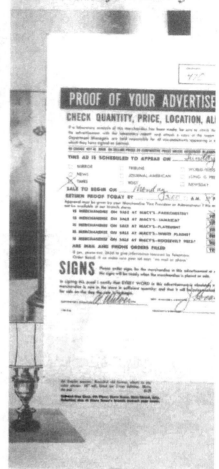

**34** Completed proofs are sent to store for review, corrections, and approval by departments concerned.

**35** Buyer rechecks facts, returns signed proof to ad department.

*New lamps from old: a beautiful story*

**36** Corrections transcribed on "take" sheets and returned to newspaper with insertion order.

**37** Final copy and layout adjustments are made by newspaper.

38 Final proofs are pulled by the newspaper and proofread against corrections released by store.

39 A mat, of a flexible papier mache like composition, is now pulled from the flat newspaper form.

40 The stereotype is then cast from the mat. It is molded from metal, to fit the newspaper press.

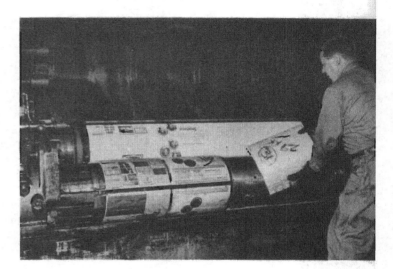

41 The stereotype goes on the press, is locked into position and the newspaper is ready to roll.

**MECHANICS AND CREATIVITY**...Learning to appreciate the feel and look of merchandise, and acquiring the ability to translate that knowledge creatively into retail advertising...in short, to be a "Salesman in Print", is not easy. It is particularly difficult when you are still learning the mechanics. How can you learn them expertly? Your local paper will gladly arrange for a personally conducted tour. When you're there, watch the linotype operator set type to a given size and width, and see for yourself the number of characters that fit a line. The engraver will show you the tonal values that will reproduce clearly. The composing room foreman will put an ad together for you and discuss proper layout instructions. The more familiar you become with mechanics, the more time you will have for creativity. Learning the mechanics is important and useful but don't forget, an ad starts with the merchandise.

# Organization of Advertising Departments

## *"It Starts With People"*

An advertising department is people working together and with other people. This is true whether your store is small or large, your volume of advertising minuscule or monumental. In this section of the book we will discuss the structure of advertising departments, with emphasis on the people, especially the graphic people who actually produce the ads, and their relationship to other people who play an important part in the ads but do not actually create them.

These relationships fall into three broad categories:

1. Merchants and advertising people.
2. Copy and art.
3. Store and newspaper.

Each group works to fulfill its own objectives as far as ads are concerned, but the goal of all is the best possible ad with the best possible newspaper reproduction for the best possible consumer response. With this in mind, it is easier to work together, especially if the function of each group is clearly understood.

1. It is the primary responsibility of the buying organization to supply the merchandise and the merchandise information to the creative staff (see chapter 4).
2. It is the primary function and responsibility of the sales promotion division to present this story to the public.
3. It is the primary responsibility of the newspapers to reproduce the ads so they are as close as possible to the concepts of the advertising people who created them.

## Merchants and Advertising People:

### *"No Pride in Authorship"*

Each group can benefit by working with the other. The creative staff's interest in improving a merchandise story can often make a better ad. The merchant's knowledge of merchandise and customer floor reaction can add depth and a point of view to an ad. An idea is an idea, and always welcome, whether it comes from the merchant or the copywriter or the artist.

Here are 3 examples of how ads were improved by people working well together.

1. Macy's layette advertising had been using "I want it while I'm still young enough to enjoy it" as a theme. When a full page Macy's-Own brand layette ad was scheduled, it seemed a good chance to develop what had been a small space theme into a big dramatic ad. It would have been interesting and graphic. But, in talking to the buyer, we were told how more and more office groups were coming in to buy layettes as baby shower gifts. From this conversation came the idea of showing the envelope of money collected from the entire staff and calling the office group a board of directors. The creative people translated this as "The Layette Committee Meets at Noon," showing the envelope with the signatures. The result: a fresher, more effective ad than the original concept. When an idea comes from the merchant, it should be gratefully accepted. How it is treated is, of course, the responsibility of the advertising department.

2. At a regular fashion advertising meeting, the swimsuit buyer announced he wanted to open the new season with a very dramatic ad. He showed a group of his new bathing suits to the advertising writers and artists who responded with great enthusiasm. The buyer asked the chief of the fashion advertising division to choose the suits she'd like to show in the ad, but the one she thought most significant and striking, the one she wanted to feature, in fact, he said she could not use in the ad at all. The reason? He could not get adequate delivery in time. There ensued a 3-day struggle between the advertising and the merchandise departments, while ways and means were explored to include that special swimsuit in the ad. The advertising department, often adamant on having merchandise problems resolved on schedule, offered extra time to help the buyer work out his difficulties. Finally, after sufficient pressure and encouragement from the advertising department, deliveries were assured. The ad was exactly as dramatic as the buyer had wanted it to be, and the season opened with a great splash.

   P.S. The featured suit became the department's running number, a tremendous success.

3. Sometimes an ad will get off to a bad start and even get into proof form before it's caught. This doesn't happen too often, but it does happen. This curtain sale ad was started by an assistant buyer, good, but lacking in experience. It was written by a junior writer who couldn't add facts and didn't know the questions to ask, so had to rely on the fact sheet alone (See Chapter 4). In a particularly busy period, it slipped by and came up on proof. A meeting of ad manager, writer and buyer was called. Additional facts were supplied and the ad redone. Note the difference (page 14). When further facts are needed to make a stronger ad, it's important to recognize that they must come from the source, the buyer.

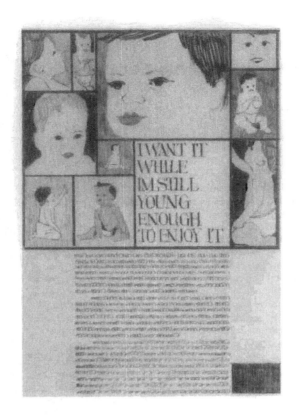

## Copy and Art

### *"Living Together"*

Since an ad is the result of many people's thinking and doing, it is important that they work together harmoniously. The best ads are always a true marriage of copy and art. How do you achieve this marriage?

Currently there are 4 ways in which copywriters and artists work together. Each has its pros and cons.

1. The copywriter writes the ad first, layout is then done from copy.

   *Pro:* The copywriter, who has taken the fact sheet, knows the whole merchandise story, and can establish the point of view. The writer can also take as much or as little space as is needed to develop ideas.

   *Con:* The layout artist is fenced in by the size of headline, number of subheads, length or brevity of copy. He may want to show more pictures or larger ones, but cannot.

2. The copywriter writes a headline only. The ad is then laid out and the writer fills in the space left for copy.

   *Pro:* This is fast. Once the headline is written, a layout can be made. It also gives the artist great latitude in designing and arranging the elements of the ad.

   *Con·* Often after a headline is written, the writer finds it won't work. Or the space allotted for body copy will be too limited to tell the whole story or so big that the story has to be padded unnecessarily.

3. The layout artist makes the layout first and the writer fits copy to it.

   *Pro:* When doing an omnibus page (see Chapter 6) where there are many items on a page, all with a designated space (1/16 of a page each, for example), this will ensure a neat and tailored page. Also, of course, when the artist works first, he can design a page graphically without being hampered by a fixed amount of copy.

   *Con:* The layout may not work for the specific story to be told. Again, the space may be wrong, elements like sub-heads, essential to the story, may have to be forced into a pattern established.

4. Copy and layout are created simultaneously.

   *Pro:* This is the best system of all, since ideas and elements and space can be worked out together. It eliminates the need to have a headline shortened (when copy is written first) or a copy block lengthened (when layout is done first). And two creative people working together will exchange ideas and produce a better ad.

   *Con:* This method is time-consuming. All ads cannot be done this way, especially in a store with a large volume of advertising. However, important ads can be, and there can be preliminary conversation and adjustment on the others.

## Store and Newspaper

### *"What Counts Is What's In The Paper"*

When an advertising department has a friendly relationship with the newspapers, everybody benefits. In the last few years newspapers have made great progress in reproduction. And they will often come up with new ideas and new techniques that advertising people find most helpful. However, it is most important that the advertising department make perfectly clear what is expected of the newspapers. Sloppy instructions put too great a burden on the papers. They're printers, not mind-readers. You'll find the more specific you are, the closer the final ad is to its original concept.

### ORGANIZATION OF THE ADVERTISING DEPARTMENT

On the following page is an organization chart of the advertising department of Macy's New York Sales Promotion Division. A chart of people, creative and administrative, people who produce between 100 and 150 pages of newspaper advertising every week. Every advertising function shown in this chart has to be performed, to some extent, by every department store, regardless of size or number of ads produced. Obviously the fewer the ads, the fewer the people. The fewer the people, then the more functions each person has to absorb. For example, in a smaller store or one with less advertising, part of the function of the Creative Advertising Director might be absorbed by the advertising manager, part by the art director, and so on down the line until it becomes the function of an artist who does both the layout and the art work. This is equally true in each area: division advertising managers become copy chiefs, then one copy chief, finally a copywriter. The irreducible minimum is the owner of a small store with no advertising staff who prepares his own ads.

We have said above that the fewer the ads, the fewer the people needed. This is, quite obviously, only a quantitative measurement. It may not hold true when quality or creativity is involved. It may take more people to produce creative ads. Or it may be, not more, but different people. Actually, it's quite possible that a store with highly promotional advertising (see Chapter 4 on kinds of advertising) may require more people because it may take more man hours to produce. The whole question of creativity in relation to the kind and number of people, is a matter of degree, one that each store has to solve for itself.

### PEOPLE NEEDED FOR AN ADVERTISING STAFF

Before assembling a staff, it's important to know the kinds of advertising properties that will have to be prepared, and a general idea of the advertising schedules, its peaks and its slow seasons. The kinds of properties determine the kinds of people, just as the amount of advertising determines the number.

Many stores prepare all or some of these advertising properties:

1. Newspaper advertising.
2. Direct mail.
3. Posters.

# SALES PROMOTION DIRECTOR

- INTERIOR DISPLAY DIR.
- WINDOW DISPLAY DIR.
- PUBLIC RELATION DIR.
- BUSINESS MANAGER
- CREATIVE DIRECTOR
  - ASS'T. CREATIVE DIR.

**INTERIOR DISPLAY DIR.**
ASSISTANTS
DECORATOR
ARTIST
TRIMMERS
ASS'T. TRIMMERS
FIXTURE DESIGNER
SIGNING DESIGNER
LETTERER
PROPERTY MAN

**WINDOW DISPLAY DIR.**
ASSISTANTS
STYLISTS
TRIMMERS
ASS'T. TRIMMERS
LETTERER
PROPERTY MAN

**SPECIAL EVENTS**

**PUBLICITY**
HOME FURN.
FASHION
BRANCH STORES

**MEDIA SCHEDULE AND BUDGET**
DEPT. MANAGER
STATISTICS
BUDGET CONTROL
SCHEDULE

**ADVERTISING PRODUCTION**
PROD. MANAGER
ASS'T. PROD. MGR.
PROD. CLERKS
MESSENGERS

**TRAFFIC**
DEPT. MANAGER
TRAFFIC CLERICAL
ART LIBRARIANS
LAYOUT
DUPLICATOR OPERATOR
MERCHANDISE LOAN ROOM

**CREATIVE GROUP #2 — HOME FURNISHINGS**
ADVERTISING MGR.
ART DIRECTOR
LAYOUT ARTISTS
COPY WRITERS

**CREATIVE GROUP #4 — DIRECT MAIL AND SECTIONS**
DEPARTMENT MGR.
LAYOUT ARTISTS
COPY WRITERS

**ART**
ARTISTS
PHOTOGRAPHERS
RETOUCHERS
STYLISTS
PROPERTY MAN
DARK ROOM TECH.
CLERICALS

**CREATIVE GROUP #1 — FASHIONS**
ADVERTISING MGR.
ART DIRECTOR
LAYOUT ARTISTS
COPY WRITERS

**CREATIVE GROUP #3 — MEN'S, CHILDREN'S, ETC.**
ADVERTISING MGR.
ART DIRECTOR
LAYOUT ARTISTS
COPY WRITERS

**NEWSPAPER EDITORIAL DEPARTMENT**

**NEWSPAPER ADVERTISING DEPARTMENT**

**NEWSPAPER MECH. PRODUCTION DEPT.**

4. Magazine advertising.
5. Radio and TV advertising.
6. Label and package design.
7. Etc.... from advertising presentations to speeches for store executives.

Since the objective of this book is how to prepare better newspaper advertising, and the objective of this chapter is people and their relationship to newspaper advertising, we can only mention properties other than newspapers. For further information on other advertising properties, the people involved, and their responsibilities, we suggest that you refer to Edwards and Brown "Retail Advertising Sales Promotion" (Prentice-Hall) and the NRMA folders on "Duties of Sales Promotion Division."

ORGANIZING THE STAFF

An advertising department should be so staffed as to handle slightly more than the average amount of advertising, figured on a yearly basis. If the staff is planned for peak seasons, there will obviously be a waste of people and money when things slow down. Conversely, if there are too few people, the added expense of expansion will be too great and there will be unnecessary pressure.

Then what happens during peak seasons? Where possible, supplement your staff with part-timers or free lance people. You may have to pay them slightly more, but in the long run your creative production budget will be smaller than if you carried additional people on regular staff.

When no part-timers or free lancers are available, or your budget is overspent, you do what has always been done in this business (and in every other business): you roll up your sleeves, order plenty of coffee and go to work. This is the time when all your pre-planning and skill in using formulas come in handy.

What happens during slow seasons? This is when your staff members can take their vacations, when you can do your pre-planning, and develop new formats and new campaigns for the coming season. There is one other consideration: what kind of people are necessary for your staff? The total staff has to reflect the emphasis in your advertising. If your store spends most of its advertising space on home furnishings, then your proportion of creative people in this area must be higher than in fashion... and vice versa. There is no formula for such a breakdown. Each store finds its own solution.

## Help Wanted:

### Male, Female—Retail Advertising

It is obvious that one of the ways to create better advertising is to hire better people... and once you've got them, to keep them. This, as you have probably discovered, is not as simple as it sounds. Here is a quote from Kenneth Collins' column, "Today and Yesterday in Retailing" from the July 22, 1959 issue of Women's Wear Daily:

"...this fall (1959) the NRMA member stores will devote a week to the recruitment of better people for retailing. That week is a thorough-going waste of time for the advertising departments. They get plenty of brilliant youngsters. Yet they rarely hold even 10 per cent of them. For disillusionment sets in after the first few months. After that it is merely a matter of time. What a tragedy! And it is all so lamentably unnecessary."

Kenneth Collins speaks from vast experience, sympathetic understanding of creative people, and good sound business judgment. He, of course, knows that there are many exceptions throughout the country and has pointed them out, time after time, in his column. And he himself is an outstanding exception.

Then how do you keep them at the drawing board and typewriter? You must convince talented youngsters that what they may have heard isn't true... and that these are the facts:

1. Starting salaries for beginners (junior artists and copywriters) in department stores are about the same as in all other branches of the creative professions, in comparable areas of the country.

2. The opportunity for rapid financial advancement is as great in department stores as in any other branch of the creative professions.

3. The opportunity for personal creative development is actually faster.

4. The opportunity to see the actual results of creative effort is immediate in department stores. It's possible to see the customer reaction and hear the cash register ring a day after the ad appears.

5. Offices may not be plush, but as more stores modernize, advertising offices will be modernized, too.

6. The opportunity, at every level, to become a real part of the creative merchandising and sales promotion team is more likely in a department store than in most other creative enterprises.

7. In a department store the advertising department is its own client, which means that they have a voice in the sales promotion activities of the store. This is somewhat different than working with a remote client... different and a lot better.

8. Getting rich in a department store is unlikely, but it's always possible to make a handsome living. And if stability and long term security are important, more and more stores now have profit-sharing and retirement plans.

9. When creative maturity is reached, there are additional opportunities, all with greater earning potential.

   (a) Administrative positions, such as Art Director, Copy Chief, Advertising Manager, Sales Promotion Director.

   (b) Free lance specialist, working for many stores with the fees based on the desirability of work done or the going price for such work in the area.

These are the facts, whether the store is small or large, its volume of advertising minuscule or monumental.

## SALES PROMOTION EVENTS CALENDAR – SPRING

| Month and Season Week | EVENT | TENTATIVE DATES | START PLANNING |
|---|---|---|---|
| February | MARCH ADVERTISING REQUESTS DUE FEBRUARY 1 | | |
| | Spring Season Begins | January 31 | |
| F26 | Midwinter Furniture Show continues | Jan. 26 through Feb. 27 | November 10 |
| F27 | Fabric Sale continues | Jan. 26 through Feb. 27 | November 17 |
| S1 | Housewares Sale & Show | Feb. 1 through Feb. 20 | November 3 |
| S2 | Home Fashion Sale & Show | Feb. 7 through Feb. 27 | November 3 |
| S2 | T.V. and Music Festival | Feb. 11 through Feb. 27 | December 1 |
| | LINCOLN'S BIRTHDAY | Feb. 12 (Friday) | |
| | VALENTINE'S DAY | Feb. 14 (Sunday) | |
| S3 | China and Glass Show | Feb. 14 through Feb. 27 | December 8 |
| S4 | Import Fashions | Feb. 21 through March 12 | December 15 |
| | WASHINGTON'S BIRTHDAY | Feb. 22 (Monday) | |
| | Fall Calendar Planning | February 16 | |
| | Display Changeover for Spring completed by | February 20 | |

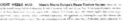

ADVERTISING SCHEDULE FOR THE WEEK BEGINNING MARCH 13

SUNDAY, MARCH 13

**8 cols**

| BDI | 150/70/21 | Line for Line | 2400 |
|---|---|---|---|

**8 cols**

| BZ | 414 | Hair Mattress | 900 |
| BZ | 415 | Sofa & Chair | 1500 |

THESE FIRST – 2400 lines – Replacing D. 414, 415

| BZ | 83 | Rondo Stereo Records | 1200 |
| BZ | 42A | Macy Blades | 1200 |

8 cols LGT #/1, 59, 92

| BZ | 157 | Dacron Curtains | 975 |
| BDI | 129 | Rods | 25 |
| BZ | 126 | Antique Satin Heirloom | 800 |
| BZ | 67 | Alabaster Lamps | 600 |

8 cols BDT #/157, 129, 126, 67

| BZ | 1 | Cloths & Linens | 1000 |
| BZ | 59 | Patchwork Quilt | 600 |
| BZ | 92 | Sheet 2nds | 800 |

**8 cols**

| DDI | 119 | Jr. Petite Coats | 600 |
| BDI | 115 | Jr. Petite Dresses | 600 |
| BDI | 121 | Jr. Petite Sports | 1200 |

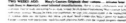

# Advertising Production Schedules

*"It starts with a time table"*

## This Space Reserved For...

A newspaper deadline is final and must be honored. No one doubts that a few minutes more spent on a piece of copy or a layout might improve an ad, but those few minutes cannot make a bad ad good or a good ad outstanding. If the ad isn't good enough, it's probably wiser to cancel it, if possible, rather than spend time trying to improve it after normal release time. Because then you wake up to realize you've missed at least one edition and have nothing but beautiful expensive white space surrounding the legend "this space reserved for...".

If, however, an emergency arises, everything possible should be done to get a new ad into the paper fast or correct one that, for any valid reason, needs correction...within the necessary time limits. The fact that these situations do arise, is one reason why schedules are imperative. Without them, there'd be more ads missing from the paper. The advertising organization that maintains its schedule is in a position to take proper care of emergencies, accept them when they come...with good grace and a minimum of emotion. It's been said, probably too often "It's the nature of the business".

Good scheduling means good planning. Good planning helps you produce better advertising. Because a schedule is not only a way of making deadlines, but also shows you where you're going. It lets you see the relationship of ad to ad, page to page, day to day, season to season. It lets you anticipate, where you can, and leaves time for the inevitable rewrites, revises, and emergencies.

## The Period of Time

About 30 years ago, department store advertising was not prepared according to a schedule. Ads were done as they were requested, then sent to the newspapers. (Actually this is still being done in some stores.) The procedure was very simple. As a merchandise event was planned, so was the ad, usually no bigger than a quarter of a page. It was then sent to the newspaper for proof, corrected, and held on a wait order hook in the advertising department. When a group of these individual ads were collected (all prepared in the same way) they were put together and sent to the newspaper for insertion. This technique for preparing advertising had only one virtue: flexibility. It lacked every other requisite of good advertising, especially good planning.

In contrast to this almost casual form of producing advertising is the current procedure of national advertisers. Their campaigns are prepared many months in advance, then scheduled to run for a 13 or 26 week period. Why?

1. In most cases, the newspaper campaign is part of a total campaign, which includes everything from magazines to TV, all with the same theme. All these properties must be coordinated.

2. Most campaigns are pretested in sample markets.

3. Pipe lines must be filled with merchandise based on the sales promotion concept: special deals, new products, contests, etc.

4. The national advertiser's own far-flung organization must be pre-sold on the campaign.

Each of these takes time, lots of time. It has been claimed that national advertising would have a more spontaneous look if it could be prepared closer to insertion dates. As it now works, this is virtually impossible. It has also been claimed that department store advertising would have a more cohesive look if there were more time for creative production. But, again, this is virtually impossible. Department stores must prepare their advertising on a continuous and continuing daily schedule. Why?

1. Department store merchandise emphasizes change from week to week (from furniture to housewares to men's, women's, and children's fashions, etc.)

2. Department stores are sensitive to fashion changes and take advantage of consumer demands. This requires fast action.

| PROD. DAYS | | MACY'S NEW YORK | LIT BROTHERS, PHILADELPHIA | HOCHSCHILD, KOHN & CO., BALT. | | |
|---|---|---|---|---|---|---|
| 16 | FRI. | Weekly advertising schedules distributed to merchandise division. | Weekly advertising schedules distributed to merchandise division. | Weekly plan from monthly advertising plan reviewed by Advertising and Merchandising Executives | 16 | |
| — | SAT. | | | | — | |
| — | SUN. | | | | — | |
| 15 | MON. | Meetings, advertising and merchandising departments discuss ads on schedule. Merchandise fact sheets submitted to Advertising Dept. Merchandise due in Advertising Department. | Merchandise fact sheets submitted to Advertising Department. Merchandise due in Advertising Department. | Revised weekly advertising schedules are distributed to all Executives. | 15 | |
| 14 | TUES. | | | | 14 | |
| 13 | WED. | Copy written, layouts prepared. Copy and layouts approved by Advertising Executives, and circulated to Art and Production Departments. | | | 13 | |
| 12 | THURS. | | | | 12 | |
| 11 | FRI. | | | | 11 | |
| — | SAT. | | | | — | |
| — | SUN. | | | | — | |
| 10 | MON. | Continue as above. All artwork completed. Art approved by Advertising Executives and OK'd by Merchandise Executives. | | | 10 | |
| 9 | TUES. | | | | 9 | |
| 8 | WED. | | | | 8 | |
| 7 | THURS. | | Layouts started. | | 7 | |
| 6 | FRI. | Copy, art, layout sent to papers on "wait order." | Layouts completed, approved and circulated to Art and Production Departments. | Layouts made after meeting with Advertising Manager, Buyers, Copywriters and Art Directors. Fact sheet and merchandise due Friday. | 6 | |
| — | SAT. | | | | — | |
| — | SUN. | | | | — | |
| 5 | MON. | Proofs from newspapers. Proofs circulated to Merchandise Executives for factual OK's. | Copy, layout and some art sent to papers on "Wait Order." | | 5 | |
| 4 | TUES. | Advertising Executives review ads for position in papers. Proofs with corrections returned to Advertising Department from Merchandise offices. | Art completed and sent to newspapers. | Copy, art, layout sent to papers on "wait order" by 6 P.M. | 4 | |
| 3 | WED. | Advertising Department makes final layout and copy adjustments on proofs. | First proofs received by store. Circulated to Advertising and Merchandising Departments. Corrections made. Revised proofs sent to papers. | | 3 | |
| 2 | THURS. | Production Department transcribes copy corrections and adjusts art and type to conform to layout revisions. | Second proof received by store. Copy and layout adjustments made, ads released to papers. | Complete proofs received from papers. Proofs circulated to Executives for factual OK's. Due back in Advertising Dept. "as soon as possible." | 2 | |
| 1 | FRI. | Production Department transcribes final prices. Production Department releases ads to newspapers. | Emergency price and copy corrections sent to papers. | Production Department transcribes all factual layout and type corrections. Production Dept. releases ads to papers Friday noon. | 1 | |
| — | SAT. | | | | — | |
| ✳ | SUN. | Ads appear in newspapers. | Ads appear in newspapers. | Ads appear in newspapers. | ✳ | |

3. Department stores are competitive. Price advantages are quickly transmitted to the consumer.

4. Department store advertising serves one concentrated marketing area, so it's easy . . . and essential to move fast.

5. The store image, unlike the national advertiser's, is constant . . . the variations of the image depend on the classification of goods advertised.

6. Department stores are volatile, dynamic, and contemporary. They create their own tempo, a tempo that can only be satisfied by tight advertising planning and, consequently, tight schedules.

## The Six Months Plan

Most department stores budget advertising dollars twice a year, usually for the 6 months period starting in August and February. Advertising dollars eventually are translated into newspaper space, so good advertising starts here with good budget planning.

It is at this point that major policy decisions are made: how much of the total advertising budget will be spent for each division, for major storewide campaigns, for important sales events. This is the point where the store's continuing image is perpetuated. If it isn't planned here, it won't ever appear in the newspaper. And once it's planned, it is the job of the creative staff to produce the advertising that interprets it effectively.

## The Six Months Sales Promotion Calendar

This calendar shows the key sales promotion activities of the store, the start-planning dates, and the period of each event. The importance of the 6 months sales promotion calendar cannot be underestimated. With this in hand, the creative departments can preplan and coordinate the major advertising events of the store, developing overall themes and a graphic appearance. This calendar helps put each event in its proper perspective and shows its relationship to every other event.

We noted above that department stores are by nature volatile, dynamic, and contemporary. Six months is a long time in a department store and many things can happen . . . and usually do. It's wise, therefore, to keep reviewing the calendar in relation to current business and competitive activity. One form of review is the monthly advertising schedule.

(Note that when we refer to 6 months, it's a plan. When it's one month, it's a schedule.) This monthly schedule is a refinement of the 6 months plan with specific recommendations for the events, sizes of ads, papers, dates. The creative departments review these advertising requests in relation to the events already planned on the 6 months sales promotion calendar. New events may be added at this point, existing ones modified or eliminated entirely.

## "If I Only Had More Time" . . . The Weekly Schedule

Most stores publish a complete detailed weekly schedule either 2 or 3 weeks before ads appear in the newspapers. This is the final operating schedule. It is the responsibility of the creative division to carry out and integrate with this weekly working schedule all the pre-planned graphic formulas created in advance, either from the 6 months calendar or the monthly schedule.

Weekly operating schedules vary slightly from store to store in most sections of the country. The differences in time table depend on many things:

1. Long or short term store merchandising policies.

2. Volume of advertising.

3. Local newspaper production time requirements.

It is extremely helpful to work with your local newspapers when preparing an advertising production schedule. Mutual problems can be discussed and satisfactory conclusions can usually be reached. When working with the newspapers, certain factors must be taken into consideration. Among them are:

1. Morning and evening papers have different release dates.

2. Heavy advertising or heavy circulation days may require earlier release dates.

3. Combination AM and PM papers may require earlier than usual release dates.

4. Weekly or bi-weekly papers obviously have different schedules.

5. Some papers have a policy of submitting unlimited revise proofs, others work on a limited or one proof system, and still others submit only a final proof (as the ad will appear).

Each requires different release dates. All these variables lead to the natural conclusion that there is no

and now...*Sahib*

MACY'S MEN'S STORE

MACY'S INTERNATIONAL FOOD FESTIVAL

Curry mild or curry hot...

DISCOVER THE DELIGHTS OF THE KING OF CURRIES

IT'S OPEN HOUSE FOR EVERYONE WHO LOVES TO EAT...ON MACY'S 8th FLOOR
COME SAMPLE, COME TASTE, COME ENJOY SCORES AND SCORES OF FINE FOODS

MACY'S INTERNATIONAL FOOD FESTIVAL STARTS TODAY...DISCOVER CURRY AND EVERYTHING ELSE DELICIOUS

one ideal or normal production schedule. Each store must work with its merchandising and creative staffs, and the newspapers to develop a timetable.

## "Be Prepared"... It Happens Every Day

The importance of a good working schedule is illustrated by the 4 examples described below. Without a schedule, closely adhered to, these situations could not have been handled. They may seem dramatic, but they are actually typical of the many schedule changes stores make almost every day.

1. WEDNESDAY, JUNE 8, 5 P.M. . . . .
   GOOD BUSINESS JUDGMENT

This is a short story of 2 dress ads, planned to run on 2 successive Sundays. The ad shown on the opposite page was scheduled for Sunday, June 19. It ran a week earlier, on Sunday, June 12, because this, in the opinion of the merchandise division, was better timing. The request to switch ads was made on Wednesday, June 8, at 5 p.m. The complete ad had to be in the hands of the newspaper by Thursday at 5 p.m. (The paper was alerted Thursday morning to the fact that they would have the ad late that afternoon. They were asked if they could deliver a proof Friday for a last look. They could . . . and they did.)

Fortunately, photographs for the ad had been taken. A tight production time table for all the people involved, down to the last OK, was carefully worked out. And the ad appeared that Sunday. If the merchants think the store can benefit by shifting an ad, it's important to try to shift. This can only be done if all other ads have been kept to a schedule.

2. THURSDAY, JUNE 2, 10:30 A.M. . . . .
   A CRISIS

This kind of schedule change happens once in a while, and should be accepted without wasting time in recriminations. The Sahib ad on the opposite page was scheduled for Monday, June 6. It appeared Wednesday, June 8. Why? Up to a point, everything was on schedule: merchandise-advertising meetings, fact sheet, layout, copy, props for the photo. But the photo still couldn't be taken on time, because one important piece of merchandise didn't arrive till Wednesday, June 1, at 5 p.m. The ad could have been produced to run as scheduled, but

it was decided, after a huddle with the merchants and creative staff, that this ad was too important to rush through. Also, the promotion wouldn't be hurt if it ran a day or two later. The pressure was then off. The re-toucher had more time to work, the layout man could examine the type more carefully, and, most important of all, the newspapers could deliver a complete proof for approval on Monday, June 6, for a normal release date.

3. WEDNESDAY, FEBRUARY 17, 3 P.M. . . . .
   OPPORTUNE PURCHASE

The air conditioner ad on the opposite page was added to schedule on Wednesday afternoon . . . and ran on that Sunday. The year before there had been a very successful air conditioner event in February. There had been no decision to anniversary it. However, at the last moment, the buyer found he could get a quantity of air conditoners at a good price. On Wednesday, the advertising department was asked if it could prepare an ad to run that Sunday. On the face of it, the situation was almost hopeless. It was right in the middle of an annual TV Festival promotion, and the creative people involved in the promotion were the same people who would have to prepare the new ad. Fortunately, they were on schedule. Fortunately, too, old art was found that could be used. In 24 hours this ad was produced and released . . . and proved very successful.

4. JUNE FOR SEPTEMBER . . . .
   IT MAY NEVER APPEAR ON THE SCHEDULE

One of the important functions of the advertising department is to create ads or campaigns for the merchandising departments to help them develop new resources or acquire merchandise for the store on an exclusive basis.

An impressive layout and a sparkling piece of copy in the hands of a merchant when he is trying to persuade a manufacturer can be a very convincing argument. The curry ad on the opposite page is an example of this. It was prepared in June, although the Food Festival does not occur until September. It was sent to the buyer who was then in Paris, so he could show it to the people involved in London when he arrived there. Preparing advertising layouts and copy on speculation can be costly, but it's a good calculated risk. It should, however, be done only when the potential gain warrants the amount of work and time required. And, of course, it can only be done if the regular advertising schedule is up-to-date, so time and creative effort can be spared.

# DEPARTMENT MANAGER'S ADVERTISING REQUEST | DEPT. NO.

PREPARE ORIGINAL AND TWO COPIES. SEND BOTH COPIES TO COMPARISON OFFICE. THEY WILL NOT BE ACCEPTED WITHOUT COMPLETE INFORMATION.

| Charge to Budget | | Advertisement to Run | Space in Lines | ART WORK |
|---|---|---|---|---|

| Check ✓ | | | DATE | DAY OF WEEK | |
|---|---|---|---|---|---|
| | **Z** | (Sale-aimed at immediate volume of a low adv. cost. 2-day response or longer if approved by mdse. v.p. or adm.) | 4/13 | Wednesday | 1200 |
| | **DIZ** | (Regular priced best sellers. Objective: one week's response at a Z level of productivity.) | | | |
| ✓ | **DI** | (Departmental regular price. Objective: to build dept. reputation; part of a long range campaign; or to present and test new items.) | | | |
| | **SI** | (Store indirect campaign, featuring forward-looking merchandise that builds institutional reputation for dept., or group of depts., and store.) | | | |
| | **X** | (Store institutional: Macy services, policies, etc.) | | | |

**MERCHANDISE FOR NEW ART WORK IS DUE IN 15th FL. LOAN ROOM WHEN PINK SHEET IS DUE**

EXCEPTION: Ready-to-wear (modelled) merchandise is due directly after weekly Merchandise Review Meeting. Bulk merchandise should be available on the floor for movement to studio, or for sketching, when called for.

Do not request New Art Work BEFORE checking file FOR OLD ART.

| | PHOTOS | | SKETCHES | |
|---|---|---|---|---|
| No. of illustrations | No. of Old | No. of New | No. of Old | No. of New |
| 3 | | 3 | | |

Illustrations to be featured. Points to be emphasized.

*Equal size emphasize print*

Date and medium in which old art ran last (ATTACH PROOF).

## NEWSPAPER DESIRED

**TIMES**
- ☐ ALL EDITIONS
- ☐ SUNDAY, 1st EDITION ONLY
- ☐ SUNDAY, SUBSEQUENT EDITIONS ONLY
- ☐ MAGAZINE SECTION

**TRIBUNE**
- ☑ ALL EDITIONS
- ☐ SUNDAY, 1st EDITION ONLY
- ☐ SUNDAY, SUBSEQUENT EDITIONS ONLY
- ☐ MAGAZINE SECTION

**NEWS**
- ☐ BLACK & WHITE
- ☐ MAGAZINE SECTION COLOR PAGE

**MIRROR**
- ☐ BLACK & WHITE
- ☐ MAGAZINE SECTION COLOR PAGE

- ☐ WORLD-SUN
- ☐ JOURNAL-AMERICAN
- ☐ POST
- ☐ LONG ISLAND PRESS
- ☐ NEWS DAY
- ☐ OTHER NEWSPAPERS
- _____ State Name of Paper
- ☐ CHRISTMAS CATALOG

**OTHER MEDIA:** ☐ HANDBILL ☐ MAGAZINE Name_____ Issue_____ ☐ DIRECT MAIL ☐ RADIO ☐ TELEVISION

## ABOUT THE MERCHANDISE:
(NOTE: Please fill in the following information IN DETAIL. If necessary, use reverse side of this sheet for further merchandise information, or copy or art suggestions, or listings.)

| ITEM | STYLE NO. | PRICE | COMP. PHRASE | QUOTE | SIZES | COLORS |
|---|---|---|---|---|---|---|
| Tunic | 23-16 | 29.95 | | | 10-18 | Abstract floral. |
| Sheath | 23-27 | 29.95 | | | 10-18 | Blue, mauve |
| Shirtwaist | 23-09 | 29.95 | | | 10-18 | and bone |
| | | | | | | backgrounds |

## MOST IMPORTANT SELLING POINT (from customer's viewpoint) POINTS OF SUPERIORITY TO COMPETITIVE ITEMS. (Use other side if necessary.)

*Pure silk - in 3 most desirable spring silhouettes as shown in current issue of Vogue magazine.*

**OTHER SELLING POINTS IN ORDER OF IMPORTANCE**

*New colors.*
*New prints.*
*Choice of most flattering silhouette.*
*Luxury of silk at this price.*
*Typical of fashion news in this department.*

**MATERIAL OF WHICH MERCHANDISE IS MADE**

*Pure silk*

**OTHER SPECIFICATIONS:**

---

| TOTAL AMOUNT OF MERCHANDISE AT RETAIL $ ____ | MAIL ORDERS? ☑ Yes ☐ No | ALSO ON SALE AT |
|---|---|---|
| Number of Units ____ | PHONE ORDERS? ☑ Yes ☐ No | Approval must be given by your Mdse. Administrator if this mdse. will not be available at our branch stores. |
| DAY SELLING IS TO BEGIN | COUPON ☐ Yes ☑ No | |

Amount of stock set aside for mail and phone orders $ _____

If you plan to solicit mail and phone orders, will the planned gross margin on the item cover all O expenses? If not, signed approval for requesting mail and phone orders must be given by your mdse. administrator.

| | | |
|---|---|---|
| Parkchester ☑ Yes ☐ No | Flatbush ☑ Yes ☐ No |
| Jamaica ☑ Yes ☐ No | White Plains ☑ Yes ☐ No |
| | Roosevelt Field ☑ Yes ☐ No |

**NUMBER OF DAYS ON SALE**

Sign. of Dept. Mgr. or Asst. Dept. Mgr. ____

Sign. of Mdse. Coun. Adm. or V-P ____

Sign. of Comp. Office Representative ____

# Objectives of Newspaper Advertising

## *"It starts with Communication"*

A phrase in a musical composition is marked *"pianissimo."* A violinist in Marseilles and a violinist in Chicago, neither of whom talks Italian, both play the passage very softly, because they both know that's what *pianissimo* means. This is complete communication.

Communication in advertising is more difficult. It's both internal (from merchant to creative staff) and external (from creative staff to customer). Without the first, you cannot have the second. For even the most striking ad is a failure if its objective is misunderstood.

## Internal Communication

This could be a typical meeting in an advertising department as a buyer describes his merchandise for a newspaper ad he's requested.

"I've got a half page in the Wednesday Trib. I'd like to show 3 dresses. They're all the same price, 29.95. Aren't they beautiful? We ought to sell at least 200 of them in the next week or two. The manufacturer says they're walking out of his showroom. Oh, incidentally, they're all silk, and notice the beautiful colors in the prints."

With this general information, the creative staff is now supposed to produce an effective dress ad, an ad that will sell 200 pieces in the next week or two. Dozens of different kinds of ads could be produced from the information we've received, but which would be the right ad?

What is the right ad? The one that sells 200 dresses in the next week or two...that much we've learned. But it's obvious that we need more information to communicate to the customer the urgency for buying. Let's review the facts we have and those we still need.

We know these facts:
1. Wednesday Tribune.
2. Three dresses.
3. All 29.95.
4. All silk.
5. Colored prints.

We've heard these opinions (not facts):
1. Beautiful.
2. We should sell 200 in the next 3 weeks.
3. The manufacturer thinks they're hot.

We don't know:
1. Why the customer should buy these dresses?
2. What's the fashion news and who's the authority?
3. Has silk been selling?
4. Are prints selling?
5. Are the colors new or different?
6. Have the 3 styles been bought in equal depth?
7. Which of the 3 styles tells the story best?
8. What kind of ad would this be: direct selling, indirect selling, or prestige?

...and so the questions go on. The more you know, that is, the more complete the communication, the better the ad that will result. You are limited only by time. Either you'll get all the information you need or the buyer will pull out a competitor's ad and suggest you "make it look like this" or recommend that 3 or 4 layouts be designed and "we'll see."

Obviously this kind of communication, face to face, is the best because questions can be asked and answered, but it's terribly time consuming. It's necessary, therefore, that other means of communication be used to establish the objectives and details of ads, so that even a free lancer who had no previous conversation on the subject could produce a good ad. Conversation can then be limited to how to interpret the facts already agreed on.

Department stores commonly use three methods for transmitting information from the buying organization to the creative department:

1. Symbols or phrases that make immediately apparent the overall objectives of an ad. This is a form of shorthand, and is like the *"pianissimo"* mentioned in the first paragraph of this chapter.

2. Buyers' advertising information sheet for factual information, commonly called, for convenience, by the color of the paper it's printed on...pink sheet, blue sheet, etc.

3. Face to face meetings for elaboration and interpretation of facts already communicated by the two above methods.

The buyers' information sheet (shown on page 24) is self-explanatory. This is filled out by the buyer with as much factual information as possible. The more information, and the more specific it is, the easier it is to create a good ad. The information should always be given in terms of the customer, why the customer should buy it rather than why the buyer bought it. Sometimes they're the same reasons. Sometimes they're not. A buyer who lists this information in the order of importance to customer is communicating clearly to the creative staff.

The importance of a well written information sheet cannot be overemphasized. Without it an ad can miss its mark. This sheet is used as a Bible by all members of the creative staff. However, it should not be used as anything except what it is: an information sheet. Buyers are not professional writers or creators, though some of them could be. The writing and designing of an ad belongs to the people whose sole job it is the creative staff, the people who can translate facts into consumer language.

Symbols will be discussed on page 27 when we discuss different types of communication to the customer. Meetings, or face to face conversations, have been treated.

The greatest asset of this particular type of communication is the chance to explore and talk through the many variations of an idea, and to draw as many conclusions as possible. But we must always keep in mind that an ad cannot be written or designed at a meeting. Only agreement on objectives, and an exchange of points of view, can result. Then the creative people must go back to the typewriters and drawing boards to produce the ad.

## External Communication

*The objective of advertising is to communicate an idea and to receive a reasonable response to it.*

There are many advertising ideas and many ways to present each idea. They should bring a measurable consumer response. If they don't, the ideas are wasted. The amount and kind of response expected should be agreed upon in advance, whether it's volume, profit, prestige, or all three.

*Department store advertising can be divided into three broad classifications, each with its own measurement of results.*

### 1. INSTITUTIONAL ADVERTISING

*This is the advertising that creates and maintains the store's personality.*

A. KINDS OF INSTITUTIONAL ADVERTISING

Advertising that relates the store to its community. *(Like a local ball team or symphony orchestra).*

Advertising that relates the store to contemporary events. *(Like the Olympics or a sputnick).*

Advertising that relates the store to its own personnel. *(Like a 25-year club).*

Advertising that relates the store to its services. *(Like personal shoppers or parking).*

Advertising that relates the store to its merchandise. *(Like Paris fashion news or assortments).*

Advertising that relates the store to its pricing policy. *(Like meeting discount prices).*

And many others, including combinations of the above.

B. MEASURING THE RESULTS OF INSTITUTIONAL ADVERTISING

Institutional advertising cannot be measured on the next day's or next week's sales sheet, nor should it be. It can only be measured by the continuing respect for the store by its customers, its suppliers, and its stockholders as well as the store's profitable development and growth.

### 2. INDIRECT ADVERTISING

*This is advertising that creates and maintains the store's reputation through its merchandise.*

A. KINDS OF INDIRECT ADVERTISING

Advertising merchandise that is *New.*

Advertising merchandise that is *Exclusive.*

Advertising merchandise in *Superior Assortments.*

Advertising merchandise of *Superior Quality.*

Advertising merchandise of *Superior Design.*

Advertising divisional or departmental *Merchandise Events.*

Advertising merchandise that has *Consumer Demand.*

Advertising merchandise that is *Staple.*

Advertising merchandise in any combination of the above.

B. MEASURING THE RESULTS OF INDIRECT ADVERTISING

Indirect advertising should bring an immediate response, but results should be measured over a period of a week or a season, not the next day. There is a direct ratio between the desirability of the merchandise (or the event) and the speed of the customer's response. A group of boots on a snowy day will bring a quick response. The introduction of a new silhouette in suits will be slower.

### 3. DIRECT ADVERTISING

*This is advertising that creates and reflects the price and value policy of the store.*

#### A. KINDS OF DIRECT ADVERTISING

Advertising off-price merchandise (sale).

Advertising clearance merchandise.

Advertising storewide and departmental sales.

Advertising special purchase merchandise.

Advertising regular merchandise with smaller than normal mark-ons.

Advertising merchandise to offset price competition...and various combinations of the above.

#### B. MEASURING THE RESULTS OF DIRECT ADVERTISING

Direct advertising is planned to bring an immediate response. It is measured by its plus over normal (PON) business, on the next day or the next week depending on the length of the event.

## Communicating the objective of different kinds of advertising

Many stores use symbols to describe institutional, indirect, and direct advertising, so the objective of an ad is immediately apparent to all who work on it. These symbols are used in the preparation of advertising budgets, on advertising schedules, on buyers' information sheets, and at meetings. Macy's New York, for example, calls its Institutional Advertising X. Indirect Advertising is called Y. This is then broken down into two subdivisions, again to make communication easier: SI for Divisional Indirect Advertising and DI for Departmental Indirect Advertising. The symbol used for all Direct Advertising is Z.

Every member of the organization, therefore, immediately recognizes the objective of an ad when its symbol appears on the schedule. Here are three ads as they might appear on the schedule at Macy's, and translations of the kind of shorthand that the symbols represent to merchants, buyers, advertising people, budget people ...anyone concerned with the advertising:

**Example No. 1**

*Herald Tribune—Wednesday, November 24*
X – PARADE – 2400

X means Institutional.
PARADE is the subject of the ad.
2400 represents size of the ad in lines.

**Example No. 2**

*World Telegram — Wednesday, February 12*
SI – 411 – FORERUNNER GROUP – 2400

SI means a Divisional Indirect selling ad.
411 is the department requesting the ad.
FORERUNNER GROUP is the merchandise to be advertised.
2400 is the size of the ad in lines.

**Example No. 3**

*News—Sunday, January 15*
Z – 10 – CLEARANCE of MEN'S SUITS – 1000

Z means a Direct Selling ad.
10 is the department requesting the ad.
CLEARANCE OF MEN'S SUITS describes the kind of direct ad and the merchandise to be advertised. 1000 is the size of the ad in lines.

Symbols and symbol words make communication easier and faster and eliminate the need to discuss the objective of an ad. Let's look at the third example again. Suppose, instead of appearing as it does on the schedule:

Z – 10 – CLEARANCE of MEN'S SUITS – 1000
it had appeared like this:

10 – MENS SUITS – 1000

This ad is wide open for discussion and interpretation, because there is no indication of its objective. Add the symbol Z and you know immediately that this is a direct selling ad, planned to bring an immediate response. The ad should then be designed to emphasize to the customer the urgency of buying. The use of the word Clearance further describes the Z event. It's not necessary on the schedule but it helps pinpoint the objective.

On the following pages are examples of X, DI, SI, and Z advertising. Note how the objective of these ads is interpreted and communicated by the designer.

*An advertising idea, however, cannot be communicated to the customer unless those who prepare the advertising have a clear understanding of the message to be presented in the advertisement. In other words, without good communication within the organization, effective communication to the customer is impossible.*

## THESE
## SIX LAYOUTS
## ARE ALL DIFFERENT
## BECAUSE EACH
## HAS A
## DIFFERENT OBJECTIVE

*Layout #1:*
An example of an *Indirect Ad* (Y-DI) advertising merchandise that has *Consumer Demand*

*Layout #2:*
An example of an *Institutional Ad* (X) that relates the store to *Its Merchandise*

*Layout #3:*
An example of an *Indirect Ad* (Y-SI) advertising new merchandise in a *Division Event*

*Layout #4:*
An example of an *Indirect Ad* (Y-DI) advertising merchandise in *Superior Assortments*

*Layout #5:*
An example of a *Direct Ad* (Z) advertising a group of *Off-Price Merchandise*

*Layout #6:*
An example of a *Direct Ad* (Z) advertising a *Departmental Clearance*

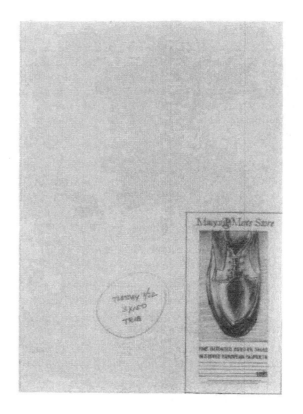

*Layout #1*

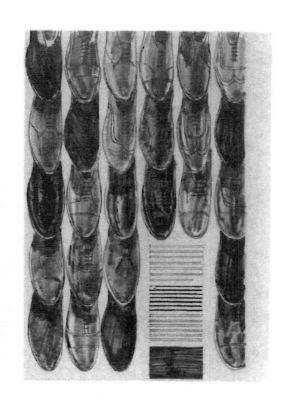

*Layout #4*

*Layout #2*

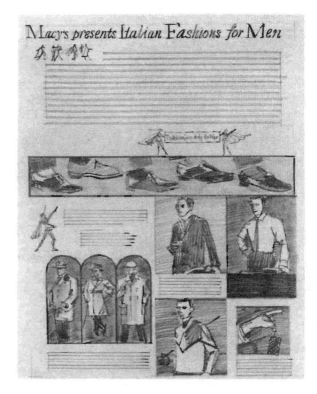

*Layout #3*

*Layout #5*

*Layout #6*

An example of an *Institutional Ad* (X) that relates the store to *Contemporary Events*

An example of an *Institutional Ad* (X) that relates the store to *Its Community*

An example of an *Institutional Ad* (X) that relates the store to *Its Merchandise*

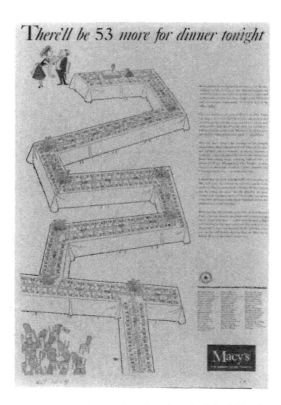

An example of an *Institutional Ad* (X) that relates the store to *Its Personnel*

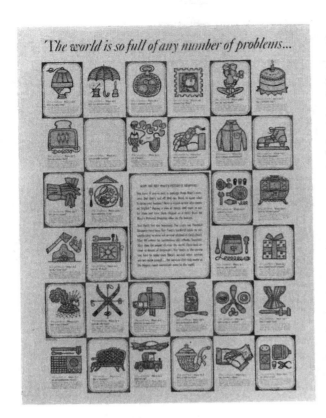

An example of an *Institutional Ad* (X) that relates the store to *Its Services*

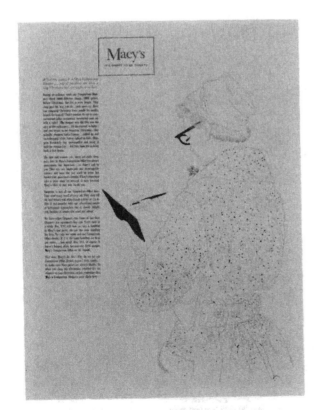

An example of an *Institutional Ad* (X) that relates the store to *Its Pricing Policy*

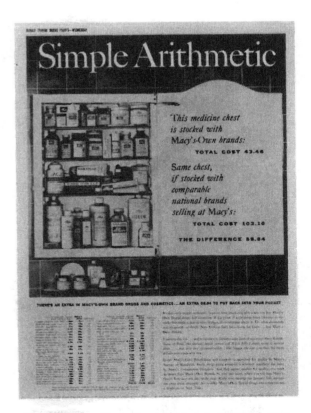

An example of an *Institutional Ad* (X) that relates the store to *Its Own-Brands*

An example of an *Indirect Ad* (Y-DI) advertising merchandise that is *New*

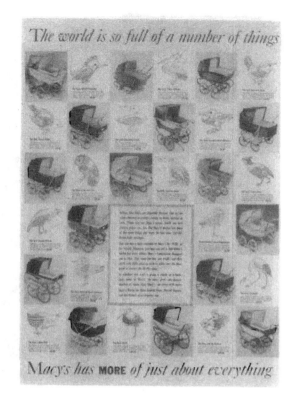

An example of an *Indirect Ad* (Y-DI) advertising merchandise in *Superior Assortments*

An example of an *Indirect Ad* (Y-DI) advertising merchandise of *Superior Design*

An example of an *Indirect Ad* (Y-DI) advertising merchandise that is *Exclusive*

An example of an *Indirect Ad* (Y-DI) advertising merchandise of *Superior Quality*

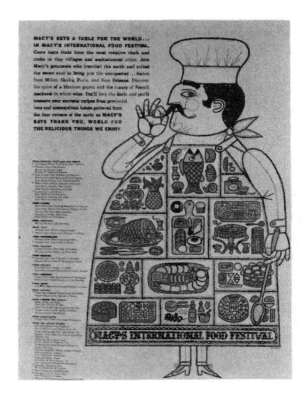

An example of an *Indirect Ad* (Y-DI) advertising a *Departmental Event*

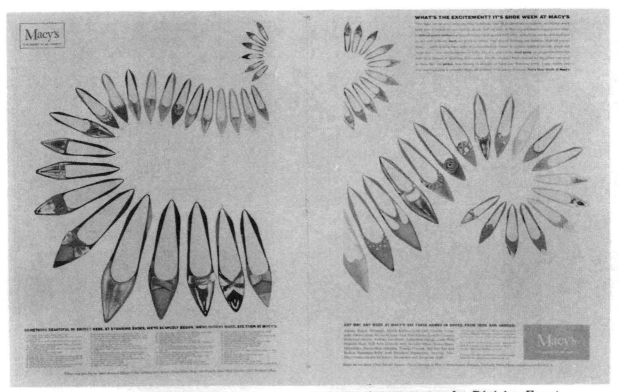

An example of an *Indirect Ad* (Y-SI) advertising *Superior Assortment* **and a** *Division Event*

An example of a *Direct Ad* (Z) advertising merchandise to *Offset Price Competition*

An example of a *Direct Ad* (Z) advertising *Off-Price Merchandise*

An example of a *Direct Ad* (Z) advertising a *Departmental Clearance* event

An example of a *Direct Ad* (Z) advertising a *Classification of Merchandise*

An example of a *Direct Ad* (Z) advertising a *Storewide Sale*

An example of a *Direct Ad* (Z) advertising a classification of merchandise in a *Division-Wide Event*

The three basic ad forms—
What are they? How do they differ?

*Chapter Five, Page 39*

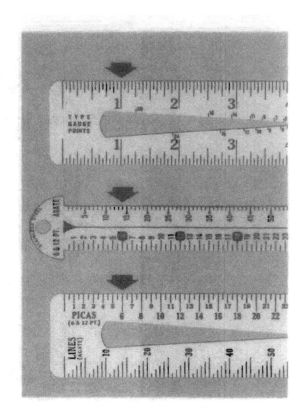

The three units of measurement—
How are they used to measure ad space?

*Chapter Five, Page 40*

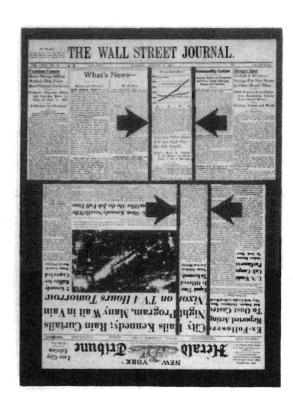

The columns in a newspaper page—
What are the variations in number and width?

*Chapter Five, Page 41*

The column in a newspaper page—
What are the variations in depth?

*Chapter Five, Page 42*

The two basic newspapers—
What is the difference in their page proportions?

*Chapter Five, Page 41*

The layout and the ad size—
Why does one differ from the other?

*Chapter Five, Page 40*

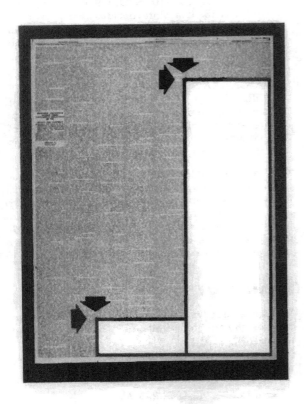

The minimum and maximum space—
What are they, and why?

*Chapter Five, Page 43*

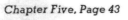

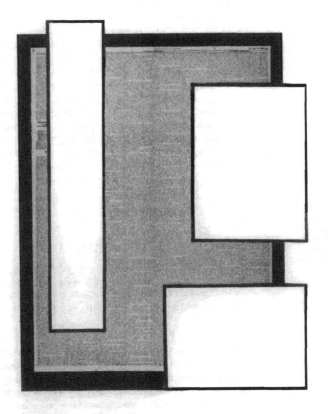

The variety of ad shapes—
What is the designer's scope?

*Chapter Five, Page 42*

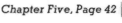

# THE NEWSPAPER AD

## "It starts with a form to complete"

## An invitation

This chapter deals with physical newspaper space, how to measure it, and the forms of ads that fit into this space.

Mathematics and mechanics may bore you, but whether or not they do, read this chapter. For you cannot design a good ad or even a practical work-a-day ad unless the mechanics are accurate. They may seem complex at first but, with application and some guidance, they will soon become instinctive and automatic. It's almost like driving a car. Go through the routine consciously and it's complicated. But when your subconscious tells you to shift gears, the mechanical operation is not only smoother but seems simpler as well...with time to enjoy the ride and scenery. Thus, when you can automatically visualize the shape and size of an ad, you can spend your time on creativity.

As we have said, learning the mechanics may take some time and require some help. The composing room supervisor or advertising director of your local paper will be glad to help you with the problems of ad mechanics. An invitation, such as the one below, is typical of many given by newspapers all over the country to advertising students and the paper's own advertisers. This one appears on page 63 of the Chicago-Times book on advertising typography:

> "Remember...the Sun-Times composing rooms operate on a 24 hour, seven day schedule. Advertisers are invited to call upon supervisory personnel of this department at any time regarding ad production problems. The phone number is WHitehall 3-3000, and the main ad composing room desk is reached on Extension 593. The composing room superintendent may be reached at Extension 419."

This kind of invitation is for you...take advantage of it.

## Buckshot or Rifle

When department stores place advertising space in the newspapers, they use either a "buckshot" or a "rifle" method. What are these two methods of using space and how do they affect the advertising designer?

1. BUCKSHOT:

This is the method of placing separate ads or individual ads on different pages throughout the newspaper. The proponents of this space-use theory argue that the store gains repetitive visibility as the reader turns the pages of the newspaper. In other words, the reader is conscious of the store and the store's advertising on many pages, not on one or two.

2. RIFLE:

This is the method that combines all ads for a given day into one or more large units.

The argument in favor of this theory is impact. The impact of a total impression that a larger, more impressive, or more varied message can make on the newspaper reader.

Both arguments are valid. Both techniques have a useful place. Some stores use one, some the other, and some use both. While many factors determine a store's choice between the buckshot and the rifle approach, these three are probably the most significant...although not necessarily in this order of importance:

1. THE VOLUME OF ADVERTISING. Obviously, if a store has many ads on one day in a single paper, it has no alternative. It probably has to use both techniques.

2. THE VARIETY OF THE STORE'S ADVERTISING CAMPAIGNS. If a store decides that it is to its best interest to mix campaigns...and distinguish its men's advertising from women's fashion and from home furnishings, it has no alternative but to use the buckshot or scatter approach.

3. THE CHARACTER OR THE IMAGE OF THE STORE. A store may wish to convey an idea of individuality or exclusivity, and will therefore separate its impressions. Conversely, a highly promotional store may feel it's desirable to pool all its advertising for greater impact.

*This decision that the store makes in its use of newspaper space directly affects the creative departments. Formulas and formats for copy, layout and art must be planned to conform to the use of space. The same layout principles can be used for each form of advertising, but the interpretation of these principles will vary with the ad form.*

## Basic Ad Forms

Whichever method, buckshot or rifle, the store chooses, the advertising fits into only three basic ad forms:

Form No. 1—THE INDIVIDUAL AD

Form No. 2—THE COLLECTION OF INDIVIDUAL ADS

Form No. 3—THE OMNIBUS AD

## Ad form No. 1—THE INDIVIDUAL AD

*An individual ad is one that contains a group of graphic elements (copy, art, signature) arranged to convey a single complete message.* The individual ad often consists of one item of merchandise and a single copy story. It is usually between 100 and 600 agate lines in size. The size of the ad, however, is not the determining factor. It can be any size, even a full page. It can also contain any amount of merchandise, as long as the ad tells one...and only one...story.

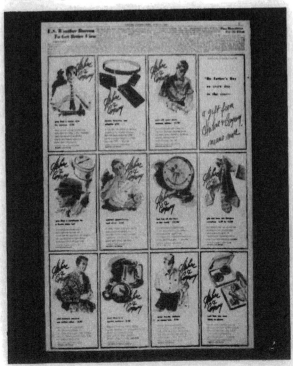

## Ad form No. 2—THE COLLECTION OF INDIVIDUAL ADS

Occasionally it is necessary for a store to combine its individual ads into one unit. The store may wish to maintain the individual identity of several campaigns. Or it may feel that the unrelated character of the merchandise would make the ad more effective if it were, in fact, several ads. These ads, when combined, are called a "collection" or "build-up."

*A "collection," therefore, is an arrangement of individual ads, each with its own identity.* It is essential that these ads be composed to complement each other graphically. Otherwise their effectiveness will be weakened. It is also advisable that these ads be scheduled and released to the newspaper as a complete and conventional rectangular unit. If, by any chance, the separate ads cannot be fitted into a standard rectangular shape, it's a good idea to check with your newspaper before release. Some papers can accommodate an irregular arrangement. Others cannot.

## Ad form No. 3—THE OMNIBUS AD

*The omnibus ad is a collection of individual ads whose identity has been replaced by an overall identity.* An omnibus ad is basically a collection of individual ads arranged in a page with only one signature for the entire advertising effort.

Omnibus comes from the Latin and means "for everything." In other words, omnibus will carry all...and it does. Advertising designers have called the omnibus ad "an unsolved graphic problem." Many formulas have been devised and some used with success.

However, the graphic elements are often so varied that compromises in good layout design are constantly being made. In spite of the complexity of elements and the difficulty of creating logical design, the omnibus ad is the most universally used form of department store advertising.

All three ad forms are created for either the standard size or the tabloid size newspaper. Since the proportions of the pages vary, and have a different scale, the design problems are different for each. This difference in proportion does not affect the individual ad or the collection as much as the omnibus ad. Chapter 6 will describe and demonstrate the layout principles that apply when designing both standard and tabloid pages. The mechanics for both, however, are the same.

## Mechanics

*The size of the ad as it appears in the newspaper is not the same size as the original layout.* The advertising designer and the composing room of the newspaper start with a production size which is larger

than the print size. During the process of production, when the matrix is pulled (Chapter 1, step 39) it shrinks to somewhat smaller dimensions. This smaller size is called the print size. It can vary as much as 6 agate lines on a 300 line page.

Every newspaper has a specification chart showing production sizes required. Be sure to check this chart before starting to design an ad. The specification chart of the newspaper will be in the language of the printer and will designate the various units of measurement used by both printer and advertising designer.

In figuring newspaper space, these are the three units used:

THE INCH

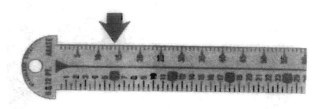

THE AGATE LINE: *14 agate lines equal one inch*

THE PICA: *Six picas equal one inch*

When a store buys space in a newspaper, it buys it by either the column agate line or by the column inch, depending on the custom of the local newspapers. An ad may appear on a schedule as a 21½ inch ad or as a 300 line ad. Actually, these two ads would be the same size, only the unit of measurement differs. In New York City, for example, the agate line measurement is traditionally used (thus the ad will be called a 300 line ad). Just across the river from New York, in Newark, New Jersey, the inch measurement is used (and the same size ad is referred to there as 21½ inch).

Here are several other examples of ads of the same size, described in inches and agate lines:

700 line ad or 50 inch ad.
1000 line ad or 71½ inch ad.
2400 line ad or 172 inch ad.

### STANDARD AND TABLOID NEWSPAPERS

It was mentioned above that ads are prepared, generally, for two sizes of papers: standard and tabloid. These papers vary both in width and in depth, the standard being the larger size paper and the tabloid the smaller.

In width, the papers vary from 5 columns to 9 columns wide:

N. Y. Daily News: 5 columns wide (tabloid).
Wall Street Journal: 6 columns wide (standard).
Washington Post: 8 columns wide (standard).
Minnesota Herald: 9 columns wide (standard).

In depth newspapers range from 200 to 330 agate lines. The examples below are shown in both printing depth and layout depth.

|  | Printing Depth Agate Lines | Layout Depth Agate Lines |
|---|---|---|
| N. Y. Daily Mirror (tabloid) | 200 | 203 |
| N. Y. Journal American (standard) | 280 | 284 |
| N. Y. Herald Tribune (standard) | 300 | 306 |
| Newark Star Ledger (standard) | 315 | 319 |
| Newark Evening News (standard) | 330 | 340 |

The fundamental difference between a tabloid and a standard paper is overall size (number of columns wide and agate lines deep). Here are some typical examples:

TABLOIDS
N. Y. Daily News: 5 columns wide x 200 lines deep: total space 1000 lines.
N. Y. Mirror: 5 columns wide x 200 lines deep: total space 1000 lines.
N. Y. Post: 5 columns wide x 200 lines deep: total space 1000 lines.

STANDARDS
N. Y. Journal American: 8 columns wide x 280 lines deep: total space 2240 lines.
Hartford Courant: 8 columns wide x 300 lines deep: total space 2400 lines.
Newark Evening News: 8 columns wide x 330 lines deep: total space 2640 lines.

## More Mechanics

Newspaper production men use the pica ruler when measuring column width, and the agate line for column depth. Most advertising designers, however, prefer to use only one unit of measurement and therefore use the agate line as a standard of measurement both for depth and width. There is no special reason for this, just custom and convenience.

For the sake of simplicity, all measurements to follow will be based on the agate line.

### HOW TO MEASURE THE WIDTH OF AN AD

Just as some papers vary in the number of columns they have, the column widths vary too. The advertising designer should be aware of these differences and rule out the space of his ad accurately. Note the differences in column widths of these 5 newspapers:

The Cleveland Press: 1 column equals 25 agate lines wide.

N. Y. News: 1 column equals 26 agate lines wide.

Lafayette Journal & Courier: 1 column equals 26 agate lines wide.

N. Y. Mirror: 1 column equals 27 agate lines wide.

The Wall Street Journal: 1 column equals 37 agate lines wide.

It would seem that by using simple arithmetic it would be possible to arrive at an accurate layout measurement for 2 columns by multiplying the correct column width by 2. Thus, theoretically, 25 agate lines x 2 should make 50 agate lines for a 2 column ad (using the N. Y. World Telegram & Sun with its 25 agate line column as an example). But it isn't quite that simple. The space between the column which is occupied by a column rule has to be added to reach the total width of 2 columns. This space is about 1 agate line wide. Therefore, the width of 2 columns is actually 51 agate lines.

This is the way the formula works for a 25-agate line column width newspaper:

1 column —25 agate lines wide.
2 columns—25x2 + 1 =  51 agate lines wide.
3 columns—25x3 + 2 =  77 agate lines wide.
4 columns—25x4 + 3 = 103 agate lines wide.
5 columns—25x5 + 4 = 129 agate lines wide.
6 columns—25x6 + 5 = 155 agate lines wide.
7 columns—25x7 + 6 = 181 agate lines wide.
8 columns—25x8 + 7 = 207 agate lines wide.

This formula is reasonably accurate and can be used as a quick rule of thumb. Yet, the N. Y. World Telegram, which has a 25 agate line column, varies slightly when it gets to 5 columns or over. The actual World Telegram measurement for 5 columns is 130, 6 columns 156, 7 columns 181, and 8 columns 208 agate lines. This variation proves even more strongly the importance of checking newspaper mechanical charts before starting a layout.

## HOW TO MEASURE THE DEPTH OF AN AD:

If the ad appears on a schedule as 300 lines for a standard size paper, the shape of the ad can be any of the following:

1 column wide x 300 lines deep.
2 columns wide x 150 lines deep.
3 columns wide x 100 lines deep.

If the same 300 line ad is in a tabloid size paper (which is 200 lines deep) the shape of the ad can be:

2 columns wide x 150 lines deep.
3 columns wide x 100 lines deep.
4 columns wide x 75 lines deep.

To measure the shape of an ad to get its total size, all you do is multiply the depth of the ad in agate lines by the number of columns. For example:

100 lines deep x 3 columns is a 300 line ad; or to find the depth of an ad, divide the number of columns into the total space. For example: Total space is 300 lines. Divide by 3 columns. Depth of ad is then 100 lines.

## HOW TO MEASURE THE AD

It is the designer's responsibility to choose the ad shape that best fits the merchandise story. Obviously, a standing fashion figure will need a vertical shape, while a sofa will call for a horizontal one. Here are two examples of the same size ad planned for a dress and a sofa. Both ads are 500 lines. But one ad is 2 columns wide by 250 lines deep, the other 4 columns wide by 125 lines deep. The actual measurements to be drawn on the layout page are given below.

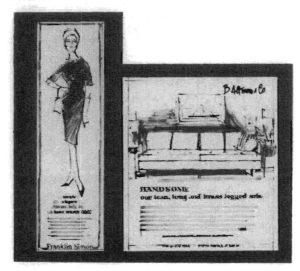

*Example #1*—Dress ad: total space 500 lines
  width: 51 agate lines (2 columns).
  depth: 250 agate lines.

*Example #2*—Sofa ad: total space 500 lines
  width: 103 agate lines (4 columns).
  depth: 125 agate lines.

Or take this example of a 1200 line ad:

The vertical example is 4 columns. How deep should it be?

1200 (the total space) divided by 4 (the number of columns) equals 300 lines (depth of ad).

The ad shape therefore, is 103 lines wide (4 columns) x 300 lines deep.

The horizontal example is 8 columns. How deep should it be?

1200 (the total space) divided by 8 (the number of columns) equals 150 lines (depth of ad).

The ad shape, therefore, is 208 lines wide (8 columns) x 150 lines deep.

## Mechanics..The End!

The advertising designer has a flexibility of ad shapes to choose from, but he also has some limitations. Most newspapers have specific regulations on the use of maximum as well as minimum space for ads under a full page. These space regulations may, at times, seem to hinder the designer. But these controls are planned, actually, to protect the advertiser and help improve the appearance of the newspaper page.

On the next page is a chart showing the maximum and minimum space specifications of four newspapers. (Obviously there is no limitation on the use of full columns). These specifications vary somewhat across the country.

| PAPER | | 1 col. | 2 col. | 3 col. | 4 col. | 5 col. | 6 col. | 7 col. | 8 col. |
|---|---|---|---|---|---|---|---|---|---|
| N. Y. TIMES | max. | 260 | 260 | 260 | 260 | 260 | 260 | 260 | 260 |
| | min. | 14 | 28 | 56 | 84 | 112 | 125 | 140 | 140 |
| HERALD TRIBUNE | max. | 270 | 270 | 270 | 270 | 270 | 270 | 270 | 270 |
| | min. | 14 | 28 | 56 | 84 | 112 | 125 | 140 | 140 |
| L. I. PRESS | max. | 270 | 270 | 270 | 270 | 270 | 270 | 270 | 270 |
| | min. | 14 | 28 | 56 | 84 | 112 | 126 | 150 | 150 |
| N. Y. POST | max. | 175 | 175 | 175 | 165 | 165 | X | X | X |
| | min. | 14 | 25 | 50 | 75 | 100 | X | X | X |

The advertising designer should also know that some newspapers have specialized space regulations. The New York Times, for example, requires that an ad for page 2 or 3 not be over 300 lines (150x2 or 100x3). This, of course, permits more advertisers to share this preferred and limited space.

100 lines      500 lines

1000 lines      Double Truck

Some newspapers can accept a true double truck (2 facing pages plus the inside margins). Others cannot. The Chicago Tribune, for example, will accept a 17 column double truck. The Washington Post will accept a true double truck as well as a 15 column double truck (7 columns on each page, plus one column of margin in between).

But whatever the ad space... 100 lines, 500 lines, 1000 lines, or a double truck, the mechanical measurements should be accurate. And once they're on paper and the ad space is drawn, the layout can be started.

**WHAT IS A LAYOUT?
TURN PAGE AND SEE CHAPTER 6.**

STORE NAME

# LAYOUT

## "It starts to resemble an ad"

## WHAT IS A LAYOUT?

*"A layout is a plan for the physical appearance of an advertisement. It is no more possible to prepare an advertisement without such a sketch than to construct a building without a blueprint."*
ADVERTISING LAYOUT AND ART DIRECTION
Stephen Baker, McGraw-Hill Book Co.

*"... like the architect's blueprint, the advertiser's layout shows the size and form of the proposed structure and the arrangements of all its parts."*
RETAIL ADVERTISING AND SALES PROMOTION
Edwards and Brown, Prentice Hall Inc.

*"... to produce an ad, one must also have a plan, or layout. The layout is the advertiser's plan for the best use of Advertising space. What a blueprint means to the builders, the layout means to the advertising managers, artists, copywriters, etc. ..."*
HOW TO PREPARE BETTER NEWSPAPER ADVERTISING
Filmstrip Presentation, NRMA, N. Y. U.

The quotations above, by three authorities, are all taken out of context and obviously are part of a complete definition of a layout. However, all three have used the same common denominator. They have said in one way or another that a layout is like an architect's blueprint for a building.

## THEN WHAT IS A LAYOUT?

A layout for an advertisement is more than an architect's blueprint. A blueprint is cold, hard and specific. A layout has color and emotion as well as precise specifications. Therefore, it would be a more accurate comparison if we said that a layout is like a combination of an architect's rendering of a building and the blueprint.

The layout is the first complete visualization of the ad. It represents the culmination of all planning.

It can be made before the copy is written, as an indication to the writer, or from copy that's completed.

It can be designed to include art that has been prepared in advance or it can dictate the kind and amount of art.

It can be a rough indication or it can be comprehensive. But once made and approved, it's like a catalyst, it starts a chain reaction, till it appears in the newspaper as a completed ad. *(See Chapter 1.)*

## LAYOUT...A DEFINITION

*A layout is an advertisement-to-be. It indicates what the advertisement will look like in print and should resemble it as clearly as possible.*

## WHY DO WE MAKE A LAYOUT?

1. To establish the size and shape of the ad, as we wish it to appear in the newspaper.
2. To clarify and interpret the objective of the ad.
3. To establish the amount of copy and the number of illustrations.
4. To determine the relationship and the emphasis between the graphic elements of the ad.
5. To give the artists, copywriters, production men and the newspaper a definite form to complete.
6. To give those responsible an opportunity to review, criticize and improve the arrangement and emphasis of the elements in the ad.
7. To avoid costly and time-consuming changes in copy, artwork, typography and engraving.

## "I can't draw a straight line with a ruler ..."

Most department store staffs include art directors and layout specialists ... professionals who have majored in advertising design courses in colleges or art schools, or who have been trained as layout artists. Some stores do not have advertising design specialists on their staffs but do have fashion or home furnishing artists who, while not layout specialists, prepare the layouts for the store's advertising.

In smaller stores, often a man or woman responsible for the advertising, and with no art training, prepares the layouts. Obviously, the specialist will prepare the most professional looking layouts.

But even those with no art training, and who wistfully say, "I can't draw a straight line with a ruler," *can* indicate a workmanlike layout that can be translated into an efficient ad by the newspaper production department.

The simplest form of layout indication for the non-artist advertising executive is aptly called "The scissor and paste-pot layout." This is a layout made by cutting out and pasting into position all completed art and copy elements. These usually come from advertising mat services or from manufacturer's ads. *(See page 49.)*

## THE NEWSPAPER . . .
## NEEDS ONLY THE BLUEPRINT

On a previous page under the heading "Why do we make a layout?", this point is made:

". . . to give the artists, copywriters, production men and the newspaper a definite form to complete." The visual requirements of the layout differ for each group.

The newspaper needs an exact indication of every element in the ad—exact in size and position and all clearly keyed. Its job is to put all the graphic elements in their designated position as indicated by the layout. In other words the newspaper needs a blueprint of the ad.

One form of blueprint layout is called the *traced layout* and is always prepared from completed art and the completed copy, on occasion even from the type. *(See page 50.)*

## THE CREATIVE STAFF . . .
## NEEDS A COMPLETE VISUAL

The creative staff's responsibility is to produce the individual graphic parts of the ad so that they will not only fit the size and shape as indicated on the layout, but will also relate in tonal values and the idea concept of the ad.

The ideal form of layout for the creative staff is the *drawn layout.* An original layout sketched by a designer for members of the creative department to complete. *(See page 51.)*

## THE DOODLES . . .
## THE COMPREHENSIVE

A doodle is conversation on paper. It is the search for an idea, a point of view or an agreement on emphasis. It is one of the most valuable forms of communication between the principals involved in the creation of an ad layout.

Eric Mulvany, a gifted artist and advertising designer, relates an experience about a *doodle* conference that is worth retelling.

He, the copy chief, copywriter, and buyer were huddled around the art director's desk. They were all trying to solve a particularly complex advertising problem. The merchandise story had been clarified, the objective of the ad agreed on. But how to get the most dramatic interpretation of the facts in a layout that would satisfy them all?

The art director spoke first, not with his voice, but with his pencil on his layout pad. After a few scribbles, the copywriter snatched the pencil from his hand to make her own doodle, inspired by what the art director had done. Three scribbles later the buyer grabbed the same pencil and he, too, doodled. Each person, in turn, snatched the pencil to make his marks on paper as though it were the only pencil in the world.

Their concentration was so deep that nobody realized what was happening till the one lone pencil had gone around and across the desk two or three times . . . a sheet full of doodles scribbled and a satisfactory solution found.

## Don't fall in love with your own ideas

The doodle is usually a miniature of the actual layout. It's a shorthand version. It should be put down on paper quickly, roughly, and exactly as inspired. A *doodle* is the opposite of a *noodle* (an expression used by the advertising fraternity for an over-finicky, time-consuming, and often unnecessarily slick rendering of a layout).

Making *doodles* first gives the opportunity to put down very quickly a favorite idea, with plenty of time left to explore other ideas. It's natural for almost everybody to be reluctant to discard an idea once a lot of time has been spent in its preparation. The doodle can be a time saver, an idea activator. While sometimes the doodle everyone agrees on doesn't work out when enlarged to actual layout size, most do.

It is therefore basic:

No advertisement, regardless of its size (minuscule or mammoth), or importance (25 line store hour announcement or 100th Anniversary institutional campaign), should be put into layout form before the advertising designer creates "conversation on paper" with the *doodles. (See pages 52-53.)*

## THE COMPREHENSIVE OR PRESENTATION LAYOUT

While the *doodle* is prepared primarily for the creative family, the *comprehensive* layout is prepared for presentation to company.

The comprehensive layout is one that most closely resembles the ad as it will finally appear in print. Every element in the ad is carefully and completely indicated in all its detail. It is most often mounted on board and covered with a colorful flap. On occasion it is photostated and pasted in a page of a newspaper, and presented in this fashion. Most department store executives prefer to see (and they do understand) the working layouts, which will be discussed later, but occasions do arise when it is important to review layouts in their comprehensive form.

Occasions such as:

1. New Branch Store opening.
2. Christmas and other campaigns.
3. An important storewide sale or event.
4. A departure from an established policy to a new policy.
5. A change in advertising concept.
   *(See pages 56-57)*

Just as creative decisions are discussed and conclusions arrived at in the advertising department, company decisions have to be made with respect to important ads. These ads should be discussed at top management level and so the call goes out . . .

## . . . Meeting: Monday at 9:30

When the advertising designer is notified that *this ad* (or campaign) is going to be presented to the store executives for consideration and should therefore be "comprehensive", he must not only know all about the ad itself, but he must ask a very pointed question: How many people will be at the meeting? . . .

Why the question? An ad should be planned to be seen as a newspaper reader sees it—at arm's length or closer. A presentation to more than 4 or 5 people is usually made from 5, 6 or more feet away from the viewer. The layout that looks good at arm's length can look weak from 6 feet away. The designer's tendency is to overcome this disadvantage and make his ad more like a poster. This can sometimes improve the ad . . . but the fact that the ad is being made for presentation and therefore will be seen from a distance of 6 feet, *should not be a determining factor in designing the ad.* Instead, prepare the ad just as you would with the newspaper reader in mind. If the meeting is a large one with many people attending, prepare a photographic slide and project it on a screen. If the meeting is within reason as to the number of people, give each a photostatic copy of the layout so that they can see it as the reader will see it.

In planning comprehensive layouts for presentation, it's wise to remember that a fancy flap or an extravagant mounting will not sell the idea (as a matter of fact it can hurt the sale). What will sell is the content.

## THE WORKING LAYOUT

"Show me a couple of roughs . . ." Most merchandising executives are under the impression that the time-consuming part of designing a layout is in the colorful indication or rendering of the type and art elements. This is not so. The artistic rendering of a layout by a professional designer is easy. The real creative effort solving the problem, is the time consumer.

How many illustrations?

Should they all be equal in size?

What is the relationship between the art and the copy?

Which will sell the idea best, the copy or the art?

What graphic format will get the most readership?

What type treatment?

What art technique?

Etc., etc.

These are some of the questions to be asked and answers to be found . . . on paper.

As noted before, most of these answers should be resolved with the *doodle* layout. But even the most experienced merchandise executive, (i.e., experienced in advertising) will walk away from a doodle conference not completely content. Why? They haven't been trained to visualize a

projection of the small *doodle* into the actual size ad. The advertising designer has been trained and has the experience of visualizing the complete ad from the *doodle*. So, while store executives are under the mistaken idea that a rough is all they want because they think it's less time-consuming . . . what they really want is a visual of the ad in actual size showing all the elements of the ad in their actual relationship as they will appear in the paper. This is real, this they can understand. This they can discuss (and in a good many instances) help improve. This, as noted in the beginning of the chapter, is another reason for making a layout . . ."to give those responsible an opportunity to review, criticize and improve the arrangement and emphasis of the elements in the ad."

The rough layout has a very definite use, even though there is most often a misunderstanding by the store executives as to what is required before a *rough* can be designed.

The proper *rough* layout is an extension of the *doodle*. It is a projection of the idea and arrangement to the actual size of the ad (as scheduled). *The rough layout is a working layout. (See pages 54-55.)*

## MORE WORKING LAYOUTS

The *rough* or *working* layout described above shows all the graphic elements . . . with the color, the tone, the mood, the emotional appeal that will appear in the ad-to-be. In this sense, it is "like an architect's rendering of the building." But, because it also contains all the elements in their proper position and size, it is also "like an architect's blueprint."

There are times, however, when only the blueprint concept for layouts is necessary. These too, are called *working* layouts. Here are five:

### 1. A working layout from art prepared in advance

There are many occasions when it is necessary to prepare the artwork in advance of the layout. It may be that the merchandise samples are available for only a short time, or that the samples will have to be drawn in a manufacturer's showroom. When a situation of this kind arises, and the art is prepared in advance, it is then only necessary to prepare a *blueprint* indication of all the elements in the layout for completion as an ad.

### 2. A working layout using repeat art work.

Quite often an ad will be repeated in either the same paper or a second newspaper, most often in a different size from the original ad, or, part of the merchandise will be repeated from an original ad. In either case the art will be repeated. When this occurs, just as in the case of the art that is prepared in advance, a *blueprint* working layout is all that is necessary. *(See page 58.)*

### 3. A working layout using mats or manufacturer's art work.

All mats or matrixes of art work used by stores must be used "same size". These mats are either purchased by stores from art services, or are sent to the stores by manufacturers who have their own art department or advertising agencies prepare the art for distribution. Glossy reproduction proofs of art work too, are sent to stores for use in advertising. Since these reproduction proofs usualy have a half-tone screen, they should be used "same size" and not enlarged or reduced.

When these forms of art are to be indicated in a layout, again, it only requires a *blueprint* indication for position of art and typographic elements so the working layout is all that is needed. *(See page 59.)*

### 4. The working layout when using photography.

The camera cannot always do what the advertising designer indicates on the layout. The ideal way to use photography is to indicate the idea on the *doodle* or a rough layout, discuss the idea with the photographers and wait for the pictures to come back. Since the photographs have all the necessary tonal values as graphic representation of the merchandise or idea, you have in essence the completed artwork from which to make a working layout. *(See pages 60-61.)*

### 5. The working layout from a rough.

This type of working layout is in its truest sense a blueprint. Even the best advertising designer cannot be as good a fashion artist or a furniture artist or a cartoonist as the art specialist. His rough layout may indicate a graphic approach, the tonal value, the position of the art but he cannot always be exact (as a matter of good creativity, he should give the artist some latitude for interpretation). When the art is finished it should then be traced in the exact silhouette, which most often will vary from the rough layout, and then shift or modify all other elements in the layout. This working layout is necessary so that the ad will come back from the production department of the newspaper as indicated, not as the newspaper guesses it should be.

## PRINCIPLES OF LAYOUT DESIGN

Almost every advertising designer comes to the sudden realization one day that the layout he is creating is more than an artistic design. It has a specific objective as well: to influence customers.

What causes this awakening? The advertising designer sees people reading the ad, and, even more gratifying, watches people buying the merchandise displayed in it. It is then that he realizes fully that the ad-being-designed is actually a catalyst, the transmitter of an idea, an idea which moves many people to react to the message in the ad. Some advertising designers realize it sooner than others . . . some never do.

As soon as a designer adds this experience to his layouts, he has absorbed the basic principles, and from this point on these principles are intuitive. He has now reached a new plateau of design sophistication where he is creating advertising for a specific objective and not for the sake of the design alone.

## Basic principles never change

Bob Martin, who was Macy's Art Director in the late 1920's and 1930's, (when good retail advertising was just starting) delivered a speech to a packed audience in the New York Times Auditorium. His topic that evening was "The Principles of Layout". His analysis was simple, clear, and so basic, they haven't changed to this day, and there may never be a need to change them. The points that Mr. Martin made follow, but it must be made clear that these are from rough notes taken at his lecture almost 25 years ago, and that these are only fundamentals from which creativity can flourish:

### "Making layouts:

1. There are as many possible layouts as there are fish in the sea.

2. The best layouts are the ones that fit the advertising message so perfectly that no other message could be substituted.

3. A layout that calls attention to the layout is a bad layout.

4. A layout that calls attention to the message, to the merchandise, and gets the advertisement completely read, is a good layout.

5. Relentlessly delete a tricky layout which detracts from the idea. But . . .

6. Freshness and surprise in layout have a distinct advertising value.

7. Make your advertising idea easy for the reader to grasp.

8. Use whatever layout arrangement, type, picture or border that helps the idea.

9. 'Kill' anything *(or anybody)* that tends to complicate the story or interferes with legibility or attracts unwarranted attention to itself and not to the ad.

10. REMEMBER: You can't feature every-thing—
    a. you *can* feature the picture, or
    b. you *can* feature the headline, or
    c. you *can* feature the price, or
    d. you *can* feature the copy . . .

    *If you try to feature ALL you will feature NONE.''*

**THE SCISSORS AND PASTE-POT LAYOUT.** *This is a layout made by cutting out and pasting into position all completed art elements (Ralph Heineman's Ad-Aid service) and by indicating the copy and store signature.*

**THE TRACED LAYOUT.** *The layout shown here is a "blueprint", an exact indication in size and position of the art and copy. The newspaper production department will have no problem in putting this ad together.*

**THE DRAWN LAYOUT.** *An original layout drawn by the advertising designer (Robert Wilvers) for completion by the staff (see Chapter 1). All graphic elements are indicated for position and color value and resembles as closely as possible the ad as it will appear in the paper.*

**EXAMPLES OF DOODLES:** *"Conversation on paper" that may lead to a definite conclusion (see ad on the right), or may suggest that more creative work is necessary before a satisfactory solution can be reached (see page on left).*

**FOUR EXAMPLES OF A ROUGH LAYOUT!** *Each developed from a "doodle". Each was drawn to the actual size of the ad-to-be for easier visualization of the idea. The layout above was chosen because it told the merchandise story best and was graphically dramatic.*

## STARTS WEDNESDAY

# MACY'S
## TV AND
# MUSIC
## FESTIVAL

### 10 DAYS ONLY • 10

MACY'S
AND
ALL
THAT
JAZZ

AND MACY'S
TV & MUSIC FESTIVAL
IS A BIG SALE TOO

TUES 2/7 TIMES 8 COLS

# MACY'S
# ONE DAY
# JAZZ
## FESTIVAL

## WEDNESDAY ONLY

LIONEL HAMPTON
CANNONBALL ADDERLEY
STAN GETZ
DIZZY GILLESPIE
MILT HINTON
J.J. JOHNSON
GENE KRUPA
GERRY MULLIGAN
TEDDY WILSON

*and*

THESE SPECIAL GUESTS

BENNY GOODMAN
JACK LAZARE
ARTHUR GODFREY
LARRY ELGART
MORT FEGA
JIMMY RUSHING

RDT

**THIS IS AN EXAMPLE OF A COMPREHENSIVE LAYOUT.** *It served its purpose well. It was presented to a group of executives for consideration, discussion and approval, and also used as a working layout for final copy, artwork and typography.*

THIS IS ANOTHER EXAMPLE OF A COMPREHENSIVE LAYOUT: *In order to convey the idea of this ad, it was necessary to indicate the artwork much more carefully than usual. After the ad was approved, it was decided to use the comprehensive drawings as final artwork. They had a spontaneous quality that might be lost if redrawn.*

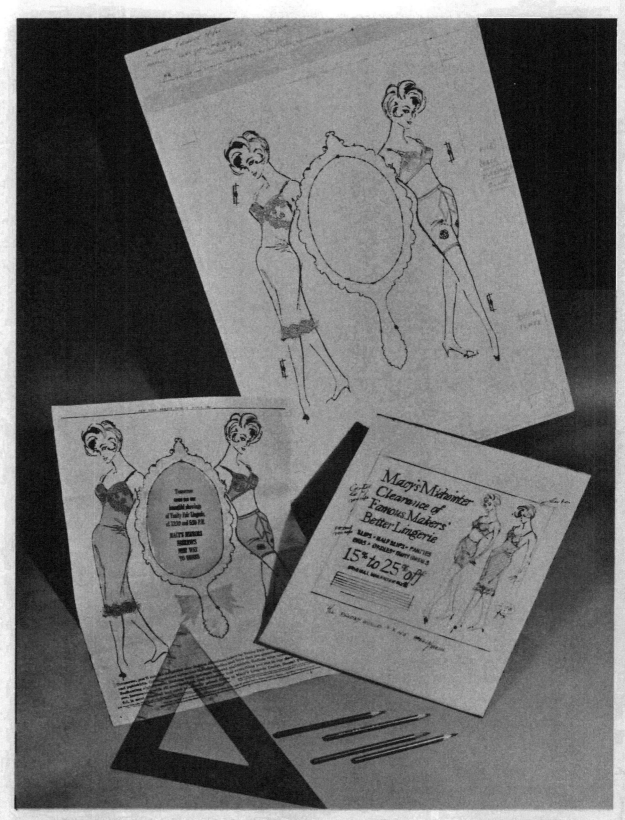

**A WORKING LAYOUT USING REPEAT ARTWORK.** *This illustration shows the original artwork and the original full page ad as well as the new layout. This layout contains all graphic elements, and indicates cryptically, "2 old ... fix" (art).*

**A WORKING LAYOUT USING MATS.** *This illustrates a working layout with all graphic elements indicated in position. Note the pencil "rubbing" of the mat which produces an image of the art for easier and accurate tracing.*

**THE WORKING LAYOUT WHEN USING PHOTOGRAPHY.** *A "doodle" was given to the photographer and all details were discussed at a meeting. The layout was then made from the completed photograph. Since no rough had been shown to the executives involved in this ad, the working layout had to be semi-comprehensive.*

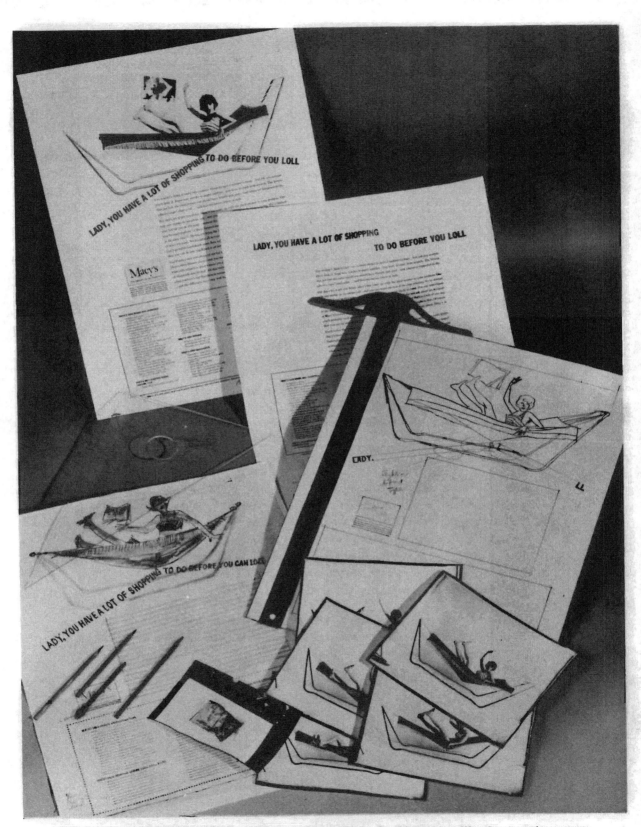

**THE WORKING LAYOUT WHEN USING PHOTOGRAPHY.** *In this case, unlike the opposite page, a rough layout was given to the photographer (see lower left). A blueprint layout, however, was required because "the camera cannot always do what the designer indicates on his layout."*

# A Department Store, Inc.

May 1, 1959

Dear Customer:

From time to time, we write to tell you about exciting new
fashions in our Young Elite Collection.  Right now we have a group of
three new junior dresses that we think will delight you as much
they delight us.

They are particularly noteworthy because their concertina
pleats are permanent...so important if you're planning to take a
trip or even if you live a busy life.  These dresses are washable and
crush-resistant, too, because they're made of a fine blend of Arnel
and rayon in a subtle, soft shade of gray.

There are three styles, each with a swirling 6-yard sweep of
pleated skirt, each neatly collared in lady-like white.  One style
has a turtle collar that dips gently to the back.  Another has a new
low torso look and a neatly V'd neck.  They are 29.95 each.
The third is a costume, a scoop-neck dress with its own buttoned
jacket.  This costume is 39.95.  All styles have three quarter
sleeves, and all come in sizes 5 to 15.

You will find them in our Young Elite Shop on the Seventh Floor,
where you always find all that's new in fashion.  We hope that you
will come to see them soon.  We are sure you will find that they fit
beautifully and look far more expensive than their modest price tags.

Very truly yours,

Signature

# LAYOUT—PART II

## ANYONE CAN MAKE A LAYOUT

On the opposite page is a letter, typed on a store letterhead.

It is an advertising message to a customer, an advertising message from one person to another person. The format is traditional, being a standard arrangement of elements within a specified size. This conventional arrangement is taught to students in school and is used universally in this format and in similar formats.

Every time a letter is written, an arrangement of the message is designed on the page. It is, of course, a pre-determined arrangement but still an arrangement. This is a layout in its most basic form and practically anyone can design it and even add a certain amount of creativity to the standard form.

This letter, exactly as it's typed on the store's letterhead, can be used as an advertisement in a newspaper. A century ago, it might have been. The newspapers of the 1800's were filled with ads that were basically either announcements or letters.

As competition developed, more creative forms of getting the advertising message across were developed. Because, while a letter can do a reasonably effective selling job, it has its limitations.

Then what are the limitations that prevent a letter from being the ideal form of newspaper advertisement?

1. The limitation of typographic size, color (heavy or light), and variety.
2. The limitation of artwork.
3. The limitation of design arrangement.
4. The limitation of emotional and mood content.

In other words, a letter lacks graphic flexibility.

## NEGATIVE BECOMES POSITIVE

It's interesting, however, to notice that in using the letter with its limitations as par, and analyz-ing its negative aspects, we find ourselves with positive conclusions.

These positive conclusions become the tools the designer uses when making advertising layouts:

1. Typography.
2. Art.
3. Arrangement.
4. Emotion or mood.

With these tools, the advertising designer can create as many different layouts "as there are fish in the sea."

## ANYONE CAN MAKE A LAYOUT, BUT...

If we think of an advertising layout as an arrangement of graphic elements on a page, then it is true that anyone can make a layout. The letter is an example. BUT when we consider a layout as a creative arrangement of elements on a page . . . then we recognize that not everyone can make an effective layout. It takes good, sound, business judgment, organization, salesmanship, a sense of drama, *and the ability to put all this on paper*. This we label creativity. Yes, anyone can make a layout, but it takes creativity to make a good layout.

## ONE PERSON VS. THOUSANDS

A letter talks to one person, an advertisement to thousands at a time.

Yet, by some strange contradiction, the most effective ad is usually one that makes the reader feel it was written just for him or her.

On the following two pages are illustrations of layouts. They start with the letter (the non-creative format), show how the limitations of the letter can be eliminated and even artwork added.

Then the same selling story is shown in advertising formats (creative formats) with the emphasis varied to sell a specific idea to the thousands who read the advertisement. The difference between these and the letter is immediately apparent.

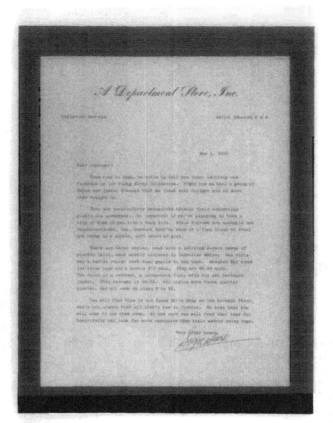

*The letter.*

*The letter with type added
to emphasize the headline.*

*An ad with emphasis on the copy story.*

*An ad with emphasis on price.*

The letter plus headline, and price.

The letter plus headline, price and artwork.

An ad with art emphasis.

An ad that creates an atmosphere and a mood.

rainbow
'round
your finger

ONCE UPON A TIME ladies left home discreetly gloved in black or white, except for the occasional daring soul who wore pearl gray. Those were the days of hansom cabs and tasseled French kid boots. Now that we've got our hands on color, I don't think there's any danger of going back to the dark ages. No woman who has observed the effect of "hot pink" gloves on a plain black dress is going to give them up without a struggle. And certainly not this Spring, when gloves come in so many different colors that we can all have the rainbow right at our finger-tips.

"DOE DE LUXE GLOVES." Verified equivalent 4.50—4.00 During red, hot pink, clover green, blue above, chamois, chalk pink, chalk blue, navy, beige, gray, white, black, brown.

DETAILS: Doe de Luxe are Bamberger's own exclusive doeskin—tanned lambskin gloves. Hundreds of women can testify that the color practically never smudges or comes off: the leather stays silky smooth through countless washings.

WOMEN'S GLOVES · STREET FLOOR

L. BAMBERGER & CO.

## HOW TO MAKE A GOOD LAYOUT

Everybody who looks at a layout sees it from a different point of view, a completely personal frame of reference. The next time you prepare an ad, watch the people who look at it for the first time. You'll note that the reactions are quite different and very interesting.

An advertising design student will be hypercritical (he still has to face the practical problem of preparing an ad beyond its design objective) and his first question almost always will be "What kind of paper and pencil do *you* use?"

Almost every copywriter will give an ad a quick glance and then instinctively lower her head to read the headline and subheadline, and to see if the copy space indicated is sufficient for the story.

The art director or designer holds the ad at arm's length to get a total view of the composition of the ad.

The buyer or merchandise man looks at the layout in pieces—the artwork, the headline, the price, the copy—as far as he's concerned the total effect equals the sum of all its parts. If they (the pieces) are all satisfactory he will usually be satisfied with the total impression.

The senior advertising executive looks at the layout through two pairs of eyes—the customers' and the store's. The first, the customers'. . . will the ad make the impression on the customer that it's intended to make? The second . . . how does this ad relate to all others? Will it help to build the proper total impression for the store?

Each of the principals involved (even the advertising design student) should be satisfied before the layout can be judged a good layout.

## HOW, THEN, DO YOU MAKE A GOOD LAYOUT?

To answer the advertising design student first: most layouts are made on a semi-transparent paper with any pencil, pen, brush or crayon that will help achieve the desired graphic effect. Semi-transparent paper is used for tracing the type or the art, or to place over the first rough so that the layout elements can be seen and then shifted or rearranged as necessary.

For the professional advertising designer this is how you start to make a good layout:

### 1. Start with the Merchandise

Is it an item ad?—Is it a group of items?—Is it an assortment ad?—Is it a fashion story?—Is it a best seller?—Is it a staple?—Is it new?—Is it exclusive—Is it an import?—Is it a color story? —Is it a combination of the above?—Other merchandise characteristics?

### 2. Clarify the Objective of the Ad

A. Is it a Direct Ad (Z)?
B. Is it an Indirect Ad (Y)?
C. Is it an Institutional Ad (X)?
D. Is it part of a campaign?

Each objective may have different graphic interpretations.

### 3. Pinpoint your Audience

A. Is it a broad audience?
    *1.* For men? *2.* For women? *3.* For children?
    *4.* For families? *5.* For combinations or groups?
    *6.* For everybody?
B. Is it a specialized audience?
    *1.* For male Jr. Executives or Senior Citizens?
    *2.* For Misses, Women, Tall or 5 foot? *3.* For
    Sub-teens or Juniors? *4.* For a city or suburban
    family? *5.* For combinations of the above?
    *6.* For others?

Each group has different interests and should be appealed to in special graphic ways.

### 4. Gather all Graphic Elements Pertinent to the Ad

They may include some or all of the following:
A. Headlines and sub-headlines
B. Prices and comparative prices.
C. Illustrations, merchandise and atmosphere.
D. Other copy and policy elements:
    *1.* Credit statement. *2.* Mail and phone instructions. *3.* Delivery and tax charges. *4.* Coupon. *5.* Trade mark statements. *6.* Location line and branch store reference. *7.* Others.
E. Store logotype or signature.

### 5. Arrange the Graphic Elements into an ad shape that will best fit these elements

For logical sequence—For proper emphasis.

### 6. Add the Final Ingredient—Creativity

Interesting arrangement—Focal point—Atmosphere—Emotion or mood.

## CREATIVITY AND SEMANTICS

It was mentioned previously (page 63) that not everyone can make an effective layout . . . that it takes good, sound, business judgment, organization, salesmanship, a sense of drama, AND, *the ability to put all this on paper.* This, the final ingredient, is creativity.

All the rules, theories, principles and mechanics that have been mentioned before, and possibly more to come, plus the hundreds of books on design and composition are all semantics. Words and theories are important. But they alone cannot make a layout. However, when you couple the words with the ability to put it all on paper, the ideal is achieved.

Recognizing that layout design is best expressed graphically on paper we use the next 8 pages to demonstrate how to make a good layout.

The glove ad on page 66 was designed and drawn by Eric Mulvany. It will be used as a basis of comparison with other layouts drawn especially for this book by Mr. Mulvany. They use the same copy and the same ad size. The only difference is the creative point of view. Each layout variation will be analyzed and described.

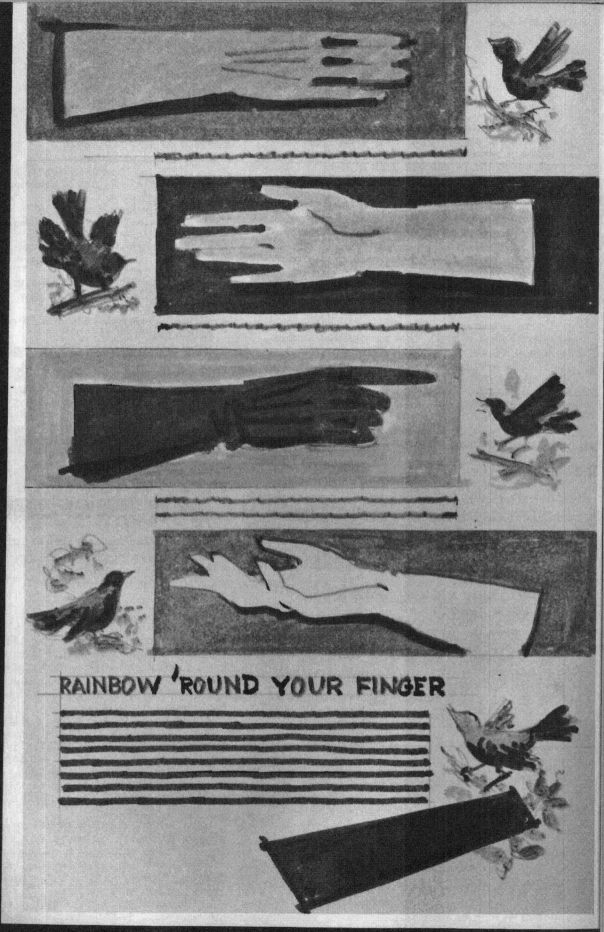

RAINBOW 'ROUND YOUR FINGER

Compare this layout with the original on the preceding spread.
This one has an exciting repetitive design and shows the merchandise effectively, but doesn't compare with the original in
scale or graphic arrangement.

RAINBOW
'ROUND
YOUR FINGER

This layout shows the merchandise effectively and integrates the copy as part of the ad design. The addition of a fashion head is a good idea—but it's a compromise. If it's important to the ad it should be made much larger, if not important, leave it out.

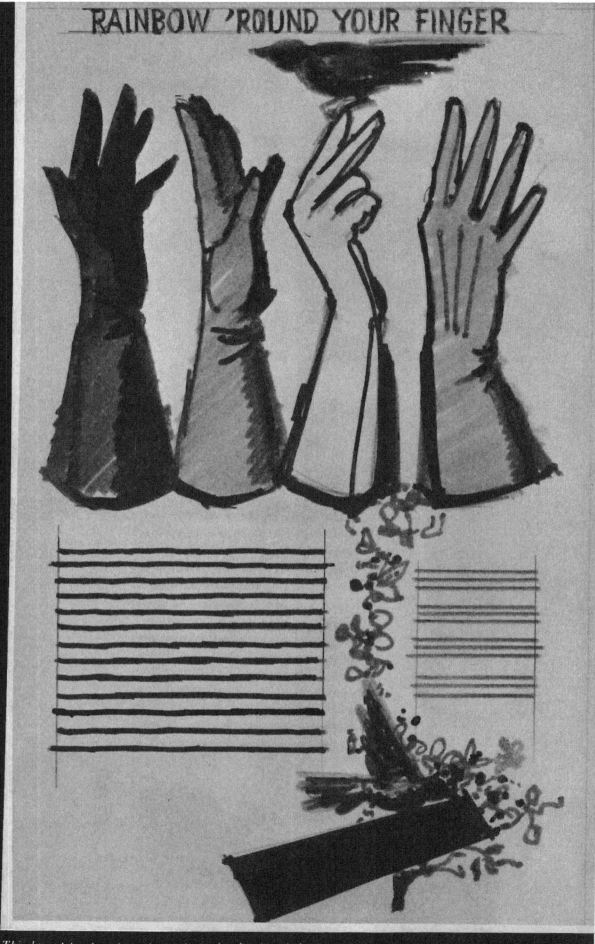

This layout treatment creates a strong focal point of the four gloves, with additional interest added—the bird on the finger of one glove, the flowers and another bird near the signature. The weakness in this layout is this: the elements divide the ad into three units of space, which tends to make the ad look smaller.

RAINBOW ROUND YOUR FINGER

This is a typical "magazine" format. Large illustration (photo or drawing) on top; copy, decoration and signature at the bottom. This is a standard formula that is only as good as the illustration.

71

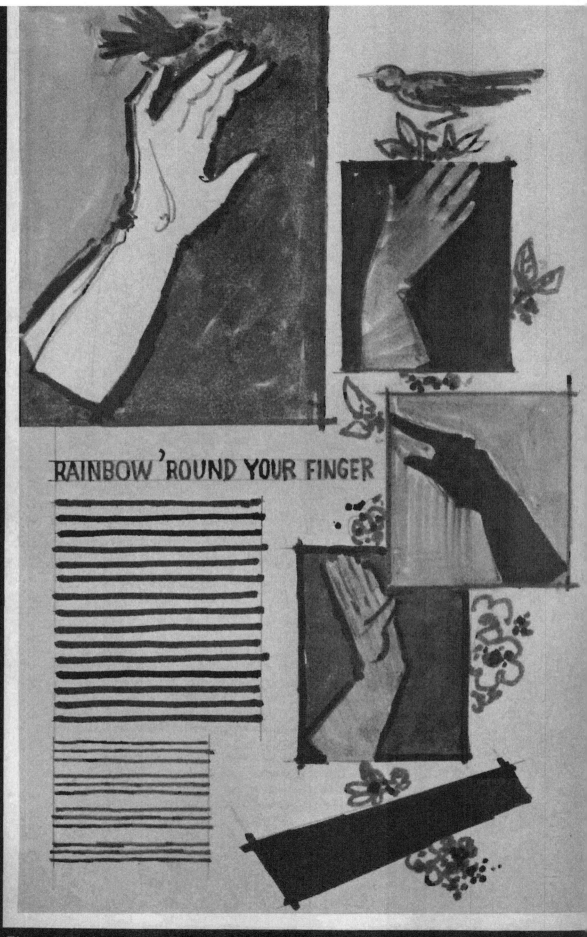

RAINBOW 'ROUND YOUR FINGER

*The graphic objective of this layout is to create a focal point which would stop the reader, and then keep her sufficiently interested to go on to the smaller illustrations and the copy. Graphic objective, good: but the focal point isn't interesting enough to warrant the space. Solution: a more dramatic illustration.*

An interesting module arrangement of space for illustrations. This layout formula, which shows the merchandise adequately, is primarily designed to emphasize the copy by making it the bulls-eye of the ad.

RAINBOW 'ROUND YOUR FINGER

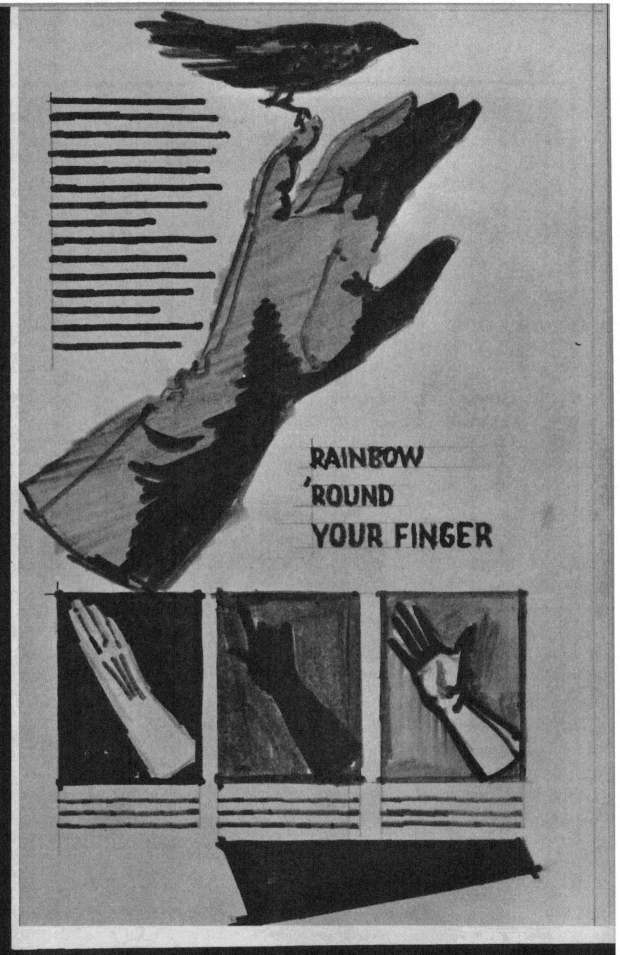

RAINBOW
'ROUND
YOUR FINGER

*This layout has a large focal point (perhaps too large). What the layout misses most is a logical sequence of its graphic elements. While it is not necessarily a rule that the headline must be read first, in this case it would be desirable. The layout-formula shown here is a good workable one...with some modifications.*

*An experiment to help solve the "unsolved graphic problem" ... The Omnibus Ad.*

# LAYOUT—PART III

## THE OMNIBUS AD

### "THE UNSOLVED GRAPHIC PROBLEM" A SOLUTION

Of the three ad forms discussed in Chapter 5—the Individual Ad, the Collection of Ads, and the Omnibus Ad—the Omnibus is the most complicated of all. Yet, in spite of its complex design problem, most stores find the Omnibus a very useful advertising form.

Why is it a useful advertising form?
What makes it a complex advertising design form?
What are the different kinds of Omnibus ads?
How can the Omnibus ad be solved?

This section of the book will answer these questions and others, and will present some workable formulas and graphic solutions for "The Unsolved Graphic Problem—the Omnibus Ad."

### WHAT IS AN OMNIBUS AD?

An omnibus ad is basically a collection of individual ads arranged on a newspaper page with only one signature for the entire advertising effort. Omnibus comes from the Latin and means "for everything." In other words, Omnibus will carry all . . . and the omnibus ad does.

### WHY IS THE OMNIBUS AD A USEFUL ADVERTISING FORM?

In Chapter 5 it was explained that when department stores place space in the newspapers, they use either the "buckshot" or "rifle" method. The "rifle" method is one that combines all (or most) of the ads for a given day into one or more large advertising units. These units are called Omnibus. The strongest reason for this advertising form is impact. It gives the store an opportunity to create a much larger total impression in the newspaper than it could achieve with the same number of small ads throughout the paper, and still get across several advertising messages.

### WHAT KINDS OF OMNIBUS ADS ARE THERE?

1. The Omnibus ad of *Unrelated Merchandise.*
2. The Omnibus ad of *Related Merchandise.*
3. The Omnibus ad with a *Central Copy Theme.*
4. The Omnibus ad with a *Central Art Theme.*
5. The Omnibus ad plus *Institutional Message.*

These are the five most significant kinds of omnibus ads, some used more often than others, depending on the store and the season of the year. The design problems for each are about the same. The difference is in the objective of the ad and its merchandise content.

### The Omnibus ad of Unrelated Merchandise

This is the type of ad seen most often in newspapers. It is consistently used by small budget department stores so they can promote a cross-section of their merchandise. Each element is usually small space, but collectively they create a major impression in the newspaper. It is also used by larger stores on light advertising days for the same reason the smaller stores use it, as well as to maintain contract positions.

The greatest asset of this form of omnibus advertising is this: like the department store itself, it offers a variety of merchandise.

This is the way this type of omnibus ad could appear on an advertising schedule:

| | |
|---|---|
| Men's Slacks | 600 lines |
| Children's Shoes | 400 lines |
| Personalized Stationery | 200 lines |
| Lightweight Luggage | 400 lines |
| Cushions | 400 lines |
| Record Album | 100 lines |
| China | 200 lines |
| Beauty Salon | 100 lines |

### The Omnibus ad of Related Merchandise

This type of omnibus ad comes closest to the individual ad in merchandising concept. However, the ads making up this kind of page are still individual promotions and should be treated as such—in headline, price, approach. The thread that keeps them together may be tenuous; they are related not necessarily by customer purchasing habits as by classifications of merchandise. The customer may not buy her shoes at the same time she buys, let's say, her dress or coat or hat or jewelry or bras. However, a related page of children's items at Easter might induce a mother to buy a coat, hat, dress and shoes to make up an Easter outfit for her child.

So the omnibus ad of related merchandise can contain *(a)* a narrow classification of merchandise likely to be purchased as coordinated units or *(b)* a broader classification purchasable as individual items, with a chance that the customer might buy them all. The greatest merchandising advantage of this kind of page, then, is to present merchandise with a common customer interest. This type of page—the omnibus ad of related merchandise—is the ideal, the objective of all department store advertising departments who work with omnibus ads. A typical page of this kind might appear on a schedule like this:

| | | |
|---|---|---|
| Children's Dresses | ........ | 900 lines |
| Children's Coats | .......... | 500 lines |
| Children's Shoes | .......... | 500 lines |
| Children's Hats | .......... | 250 lines |
| Children's Jewelry | ........ | 150 lines |
| Children's Gloves | .......... | 100 lines |

## The Omnibus ad with a Central Copy Theme

This omnibus ad grouping can contain either related or unrelated merchandise. Its common denominator is the copy approach. Each ad on the page is written to conform to, or elaborate on, a specific point of view that is repeated—and, by repetition, dramatized. The page could contain a general editorial idea that sets the pace, and the copy on the individual ads then picks up and repeats the basic theme in a variety of ways. Some of the editorial ideas are based on the following:

1. Order by mail or phone.
2. Import merchandise story.
3. Department event or show.
4. For the bride.
6. For Mother's Day or Father's Day.
6. Storewide sale.
7. Credit accounts.
   etc., etc.

A typical page of this kind might appear on a schedule as shown below, but space will seldom be scheduled for a general editorial. The editorial space will have to be taken from the total area scheduled for the omnibus page.

| | | |
|---|---|---|
| Hand Screened Blankets | .... | 1000 lines |
| Bath Towels | .............. | 400 lines |
| Muslin Sheets | .......... | 300 lines |
| Belgian Linen | ............. | 300 lines |
| Blanket Irregulars | ........ | 400 lines |

## The Omnibus ad with a Central Art Theme

This group of ads is similar to the omnibus with a central copy idea. It might very well have a central copy idea as well. Its distinguishing characteristic, or the common denominator, is a graphic idea that is repeated in one way or another throughout the page—over and above the merchandise illustrations. This art, or decoration, gives the page a unified look and should be used to enhance the individual items, not to submerge them. The most obvious use of the art idea is in Christmas advertising. Here are some others used by most stores:

1. Easter.
2. Special storewide promotions.
3. Mother's or Father's Day.
4. White sales.

A typical page of this kind might appear on a schedule like this:

| | | |
|---|---|---|
| Electricals | ............... | 800 lines |
| Hotray | .................... | 500 lines |
| Spice Rack with Spices | ..... | 200 lines |
| Canister Set | ............ | 200 lines |
| Folding Game Table | ....... | 200 lines |
| Electric Plate Warmer | ...... | 100 lines |
| Salt and Pepper Set | ........ | 100 lines |
| Steak Set and Decanter | ..... | 300 lines |

## The Omnibus ad plus an Institutional Message

This type of omnibus ad gives the store an opportunity to tell a variety of messages in relatively small space. The store can also achieve continuity and repeated impressions of an institutional or storewide message. These messages do not necessarily have to be related to the merchandise in the rest of the ad. In some cases, however, they may. Actually the institutional message can be added to any of the four forms of omnibus ads discussed above . . . and be a further way of unifying it. The ad shown on page 84 is an example of an omnibus with an Institutional message that has no direct relationship to the merchandise. Its objective was to help build an audience for a Fashion Show on TV. The space for this editorial did not appear on the schedule, but a pre-planning session in the advertising department made the necessary arrangements for the space before the ad went to work.

A Fashion Show audience build-up is only one of many, many subjects used in this way. Here are a few of the obvious ones:

1. Special night openings.
2. Store credit.
3. Mail and telephone emphasis.
4. Parking.
5. Branch store emphasis.
6. Special department events.
7. New shops or special window displays.

This ad appeared on the schedule like this:

| | | |
|---|---|---|
| Fabric Sale | .............. | 1300 lines |
| Fabric Fashion Show | ...... | 200 lines |
| Paisley Culotte Dress | ...... | 600 lines |
| Famous Name Pump | ....... | 300 lines |

## WHY IS THE OMNIBUS A COMPLEX ADVERTISING FORMAT?

Any experienced advertising designer will tell you that the easiest ad to design is the Individual ad. The elements are relatively few and controllable both in color and size. He will also tell you that an interesting arrangement, a focal point, and the proper sequence of the graphic elements do not have to be forced. Another reason why the Individual ad is easier to design is that the designer is usually working with one buyer and one copywriter and that agreement on emphasis can be reached much more readily.

Now multiply the relatively simple problems of the Individual ad by four, five, or more times and you have the complex problem of the omnibus:

1. Each ad in the omnibus page may have its own writer.
2. Each ad may have its own buyer with his own point of view.
3. Each ad has its own merchandise story to be told in a way that best fits the story.
4. Each ad has its own shape to fit its own elements.
5. Each ad has its own artwork or perhaps no art at all.

6. Each ad should have its own focal point.
7. Each ad should have its own logical sequence of elements.
8. Each ad should have its own interesting arrangement.

Even if all the individual ads were masterfully designed as separate ads, and were all put together on a page (if they could fit together in one page), they would not make a good over-all page impression. It's like 5 or 6 singers, each with a beautiful voice, singing the same tune—but each interpreting it in his own way. The result is discord, even though each voice—if you could listen to it separately—would be lovely. However, under the control of a choral director, who holds back some voices and lets others sing out, and establishes one tempo, one interpretation, the maximum musical impression of the song is brought out. And so it is with an omnibus page, and its own choir master—the designer. He must be able to blend the ads to achieve a cohesive design. *The characteristics of the individual ads must be submerged or exaggerated for the good of the entire page.* Harmony must be created by the control of all the elements:

1. The entire page must have one focal point.
2. The entire page must have logical sequence.
3. The entire page must have interesting arrangement.
4. The entire page must have simplicity of design.

If this sounds insurmountable, it's not: good omnibus pages are being designed every day by many stores throughout the country. Formulas and rules have been devised that make it possible to create good omnibus ads. Here are some:

## YOU CAN'T DESIGN AN OMNIBUS AD WITH A SLIDE RULE

### Space Flexibility

An advertising designer's responsibility to honor the space requested for an ad is a paramount obligation. He may make the ad smaller, if all the space requested is not necessary, but he should not arbitrarily make it larger. Increasing the size of an ad without prior discussion and agreement can cause serious budget problems. However, when the designer works on an omnibus ad, he must have some space flexibility. In order to improve the organization of the page, he may have to make some ads larger and some smaller. This may cause some space budget problems within the page, but the total space requested should not be greater than the total space originally scheduled. There must be a controllable factor in the amount of space freedom the designer can have. A good rule is a 10% to 15% linage increase or decrease in the space of any ad in an omnibus page—not more.

### Artwork Flexibility

The designer can usually control the position of the art in an omnibus ad, but he doesn't have control of the number of illustrations requested. The color of the art is determined by the merchandise. The number of illustrations is usually determined by the advertising event.

Since the designer can control the position of the art in the layout, the first part of this three-way problem is solved. The second part of the problem lies in the ability of the designer to integrate the color of the merchandise art into the layout. This is not easy. It requires ingenuity and creativity—but it can be done.

The last third of the problem — controlling the number of illustrations—requires persuasion, salesmanship, perseverance, and good business judgment.

It takes ability to persuade the other people involved in the ad that the ad would be a better one if the number of illustrations were fewer . . . or more. The designer should not expect to win this argument every time, but an "A" for effort may help with the same buyer on the next problem ad. The designer should never base his argument for fewer illustrations on the merits of artistic design alone. It's not valid. But the argument can be based on good sound business judgment; namely, that three small illustrations (as an example) with detail lacking, may sell less than two larger illustrations. On the other hand, good design should not be apologized for, especially when it's coupled with a good business decision. The two usually go hand in hand and will result in a better ad.

### Copy Flexibility

In large advertising departments, it's possible that the copy for an omnibus page will be written before the layout is made, and that the copy may be written by two, three, or more copywriters. These writers realize that each ad is part of an omnibus page because it appears that way on the schedule. What they don't know is the graphic relationship of ad to ad within the omnibus. It's the designer's problem to relate these ads in his layout. His obligation is first to make the copy elements fit. If they can't, he should then discuss the ad with the writers and *suggest* they modify the number of copy elements (the fewer elements in an omnibus the better) and "please, can't you cut the copy?" If this can't be accomplished in a polite discussion, then the problem has to be resolved by a higher authority in the advertising department *before* tempers are aroused and fur flies. The higher authority (copy chief, art director, advertising manager, etc.) may rule for the layout, for the copy, or, like Solomon, find a compromise.

## HOW TO DESIGN A GOOD OMNIBUS AD

### How are you going to keep them in the page?

The designer's first concern in creating an omnibus ad is to attract the reader to the page or part of the page, and then to keep the reader looking at it as long as possible. This is not quite as difficult as it seems to be. Actually, readers of newspapers have created their own reading habits, or the papers have traditionally created such habits for them. It's just a matter of taking advantage of these reading habits for the purpose of design.

Almost every standard size newspaper in English-speaking countries starts with a major headline at the top of the page, which reads from left to right, then leads the reader into the rest of the news story in the outside or right hand columns of the paper. The story then continues down the column till its conclusion. If the headline is news and interests the reader, the first important objective has been accomplished:

*The reader has been attracted to the page*

If the details of the story are interesting, and the story read, objective number two has been accomplished:

*The reader has been kept on the page*

The third objective is more difficult: *How long can you keep the reader on the page?* Obviously, the more interesting the news on the page, the more time the reader will spend on it. But this news should be presented in a dramatic way to insure attention. Newspapers do this with photographs, change of typographic pace, or a combination of both. Designing an omnibus page is no different from designing page one of a newspaper. The elements are different, the look of the pages different, But The Objectives Are The Same:

1. To attract the reader to the page.
2. To lead the reader through the page.
3. To keep the reader on the page (as long as possible before turning to the comics).

Two graphic formulas are available to advertising designers for omnibus ads and, when used properly, can attain the objectives above. Both formulas allow for infinite variations. Both formulas are derived from the front page of the standard size newspaper. These formulas can be used independently or together. They are the basis of good omnibus advertising design:

1. The FLOW formula for omnibus ads.
2. The MODULE formula for omnibus ads.

Combine the two formulas in the same ad, and you approach the ideal omnibus ad.

## THE FLOW FORMULA

*The Flow Formula is based on the natural habits of the newspaper reader. It's a graphic plan devised to attract and lead the reader through the page.*

The illustrations on pages 86-89 show the application of the Flow Formula—from newspaper page to an "eye flow" diagram to the omnibus layout. The possibilities of layout variations based on this formula are unlimited. This is fortunate, since space and merchandise requirements vary radically with every omnibus page.

## THE MODULE FORMULA

*The Module Formula is based on the space arrangement of the newspaper page. It's a graphic plan that subdivides the page into logical working areas.*

Standard newspaper pages are divided into 6, 7, 8, or 9 columns. This is the newspaper's vertical unit of measurement. This column is the module. For purposes of standardization and easy reading, the newspaper will almost always use column units for its news and pictorial stories.

Omnibus pages, too, can be based on a module arrangement for their space breakdown.

The advertising designer must go one step further. He should use not only a vertical module, but a horizontal module as well.

The illustrations on pages 90-95 show the application of the Module Formula—from the newspaper page to an omnibus page layout, as well as other space arrangements. The possibility of space variations are infinite, but the important point to remember is that the best space variations and resultant layouts occur when . . . *all vertical lines are vertical from the top of the page to the bottom, and all horizontal lines horizontal from side to side.* A broken line, either from top to bottom or from side to side, will further complicate the design of the omnibus page, which is in itself complex.

## THE FLOW PLUS THE MODULE— THE ULTIMATE OMNIBUS FORMULA

Some stores prefer the Flow Formula for their omnibus pages because it permits them to advertise many items and still maintain the appearance of an individual ad. Other stores prefer the flexibility of the Module Formula. The advantages of both can be achieved when the two formulas are combined.

The next illustrations show how an effective omnibus page can be designed when one formula is superimposed on the other. *(Pages 96, 97, 98, 99.)*

## THE OMNIBUS FOR THE TABLOID SIZE PAGE

The Flow Formula is not easily adapted to the tabloid size page. You don't need it because, since the page is smaller, the reader's eye can span the entire page with very little effort. The Module arrangement however, is ideal. It adapts itself readily and naturally and is a very effective formula for tabloid omnibus designs. Mr. Greiss, an experienced advertising designer and administrator, spent a long time studying the problem of the tabloid omnibus and decided that the module arrangement was the ideal formula for this kind of page because of its size and scale. He prepared a number of formats to be used by his staff, which have worked very well. Some of them are shown on pages 100, 101, 102, 103, 104 and 105. Note how simple, clean, and flexible they are.

This is an example of an omnibus ad of unrelated merchandise. Each ad in the page has been designed to retain its own individuality and readership, yet the page is still effective as a complete unit of design.

**THIS IS AN EXAMPLE OF AN OMNIBUS AD OF RELATED MERCHANDISE.** *It comes closest to the individual ad in merchandising concept. However, the ads are still individual promotions and should be treated as such—in headlines, prices and approach.*

**THIS IS AN EXAMPLE OF AN OMNIBUS PAGE WITH A CENTRAL COPY THEME.** *It contains a general editorial idea that sets the pace, and the copy in the individual ads then picks up and repeats the basic theme.*

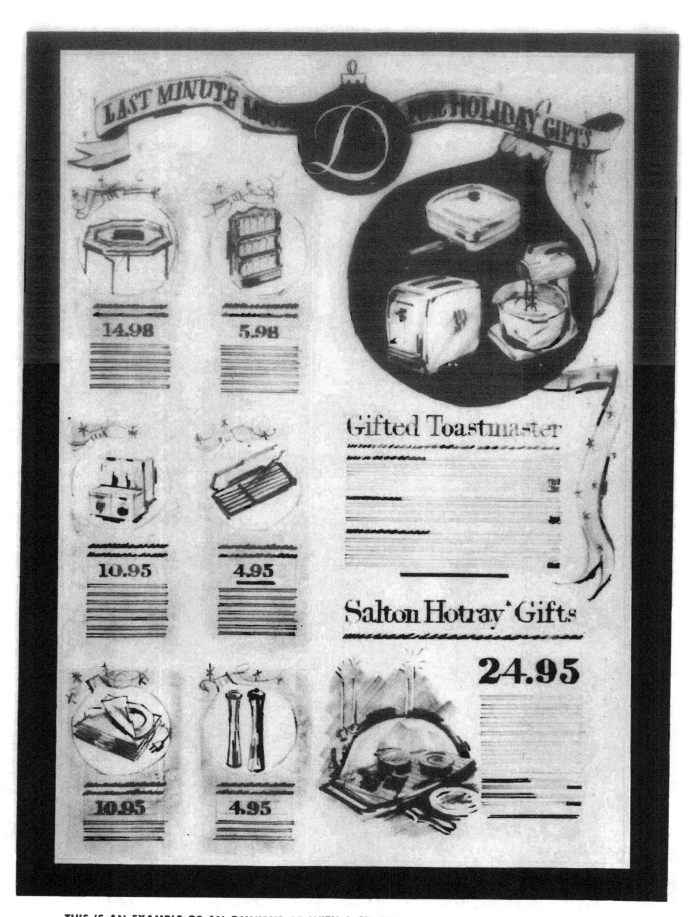

**THIS IS AN EXAMPLE OF AN OMNIBUS AD WITH A CENTRAL ART THEME.** *This art, or decoration gives the page a unified look and should be used to enhance the individual items, not to submerge them.*

**THIS IS AN EXAMPLE OF AN OMNIBUS AD PLUS AN INSTITUTIONAL MESSAGE.** *This type of ad gives the store an opportunity to tell a variety of messages, related or unrelated to the merchandise in small—but important—space.*

# NEW YORK
# Herald Tribune
### Late City Edition

A European Edition Is Published Daily in Paris

120th Year     FRIDAY, DECEMBER 30, 1960     FIVE CENTS

## Central Appeals For 10% Rise in Commuter Fare

Request to P. S. C. Also Calls For Coach-Fare Rise; Tax Relief Asked

By Robert K. Bird

## East, West Germans in Trade Pact

Berlin Question Left Unsettled

## King Baudouin Flies Home As Belgian Crisis Worsens

CRISIS ENDS HONEYMOON—Belgian King Baudouin and his bride of two weeks, Queen Fabiola, riding in car from airport to Laeken Palace, their Brussels residence, yesterday on return from honeymoon in Spain.

## Police Rout Strikers in Main Cities

Riots Interrupt The Honeymoon

By Gaston Coblentz

## Rockefeller Sets War on Joblessness

$100 Million For Loans to Firms

By Charles N. Quinn

## Red China Reports Sixth Of Farm Area Ravaged

Droughts, Typhoons, Insects And Floods 'Worst in Last 100 Years'

TOKYO, Dec. 29

## Behind Belgian Crisis

### The Old Flemish-Walloon Feud

### Opponent Quotes Bard in Vain

## Papp's Shakespeare Wins Entree to High Schools

By James J. Morrisroe

Joseph Papp

## F.B.I. Proposes New Name: 'Teen Brigands'

WASHINGTON, Dec. 29

## Kennedy Plans a Roving Ambassador—Harriman?

By David Wise
PALM BEACH, Fla., Dec. 29

## Bank Clerk on 11th Floor Shot By Builders' Rivet Gun Across Street

By Joel Seldin

## De Sapio Breaks Grip Of Mayor on Jack's Post

By Tom O'Hara

### Say He Errs on Religious Law

## City Jews Hit at Ben-Gurion For Attack on U. S. Judaism

By Martin C. Berck

## Margaret to Fly Tourist Class

LONDON, Dec. 29 (AP)

## INDEX

..."The Flow Formula is based on the natural habits of the newspaper reader. It's a graphic plan devised to attract and lead the reader through the page"...

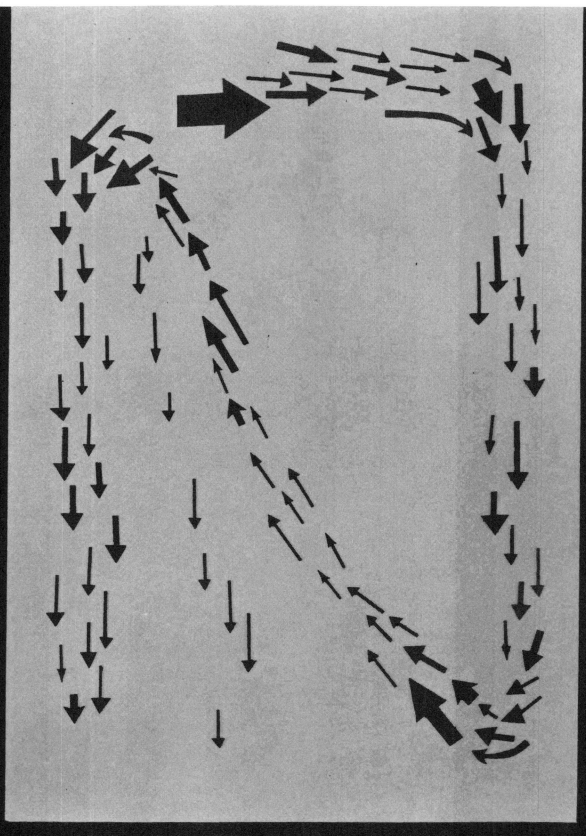

**THE FLOW FORMULA PATTERN IS USED HERE AS THE BASIS FOR AN OMNIBUS AD.** *The possibilities of layout variations using this formula are unlimited. Some stores prefer the Flow Formula without Module rule separators (as shown on the right) because it permits them to advertise many items and still maintain the appearance of an individual ad.*

..."Standard newspaper pages are divided into 6, 7, 8 or 9 columns. This is the newspaper's vertical unit of measurement. This column is the module."...

*. . ."The Module Formula is based on the space arrangement of the newspaper page. It's a graphic plan that subdivides the page into logical working areas."*

This diagram shows the 8 column rules accented for emphasis creating the first part of the module arrangement.

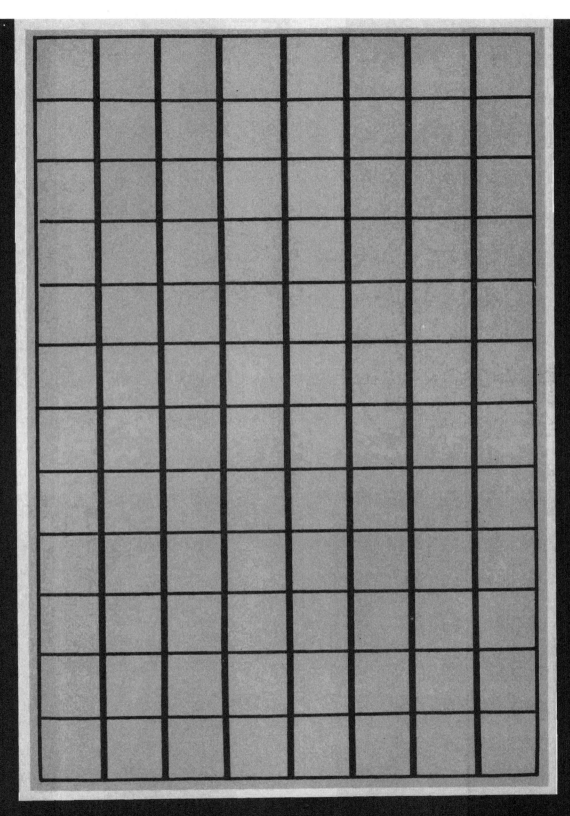

*The module arrangement is now complete. See the next 2 pages for advertising space arrangements based on this formula.*

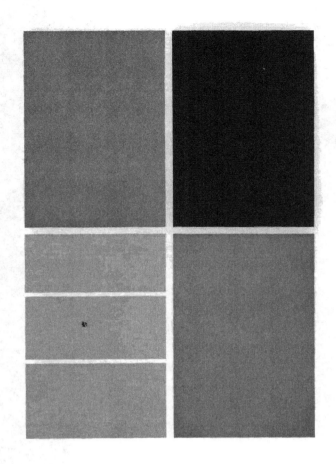

**MODULE ARRANGEMENT FOR STANDARD OMNIBUS PAGE:** *Each diagram represents a full page in a standard size newspaper. The module shapes represent the ad space requested on the advertising schedule. Since an omnibus ad is in itself a complex design problem, it's wise to organize the spaces in simple rather than the complex forms shown to the left. Note, too, that the major spaces are separated by wider margins and the secondary spaces by narrower margins. This gives each ad its own unit of space and yet does not break the page visually into too many units. The most practical rule to follow, when dividing the omnibus page into advertising areas, is to keep as many margins as possible horizontal from side to side, and vertical from top to bottom, with the fewest number of breaks.*

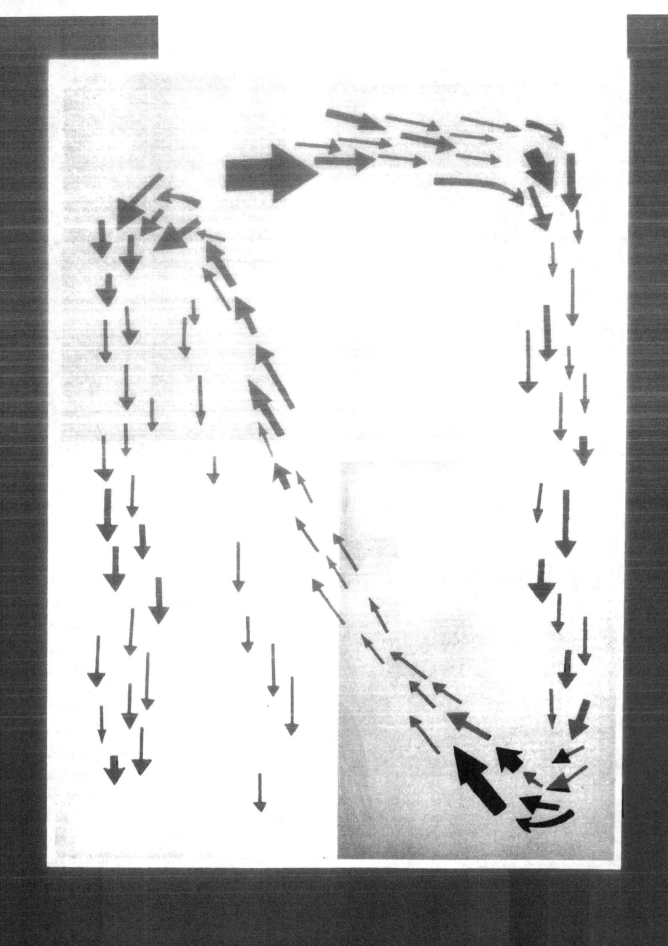

*This is an omnibus layout based on the combined Flow and Module formula shown on the opposite page. Arthur Hirschhorn, an experienced and extremely talented advertising designer (who designed most of the omnibus pages especially for this book) shows here how the spirit of the design can be achieved even in the first rough layout.*

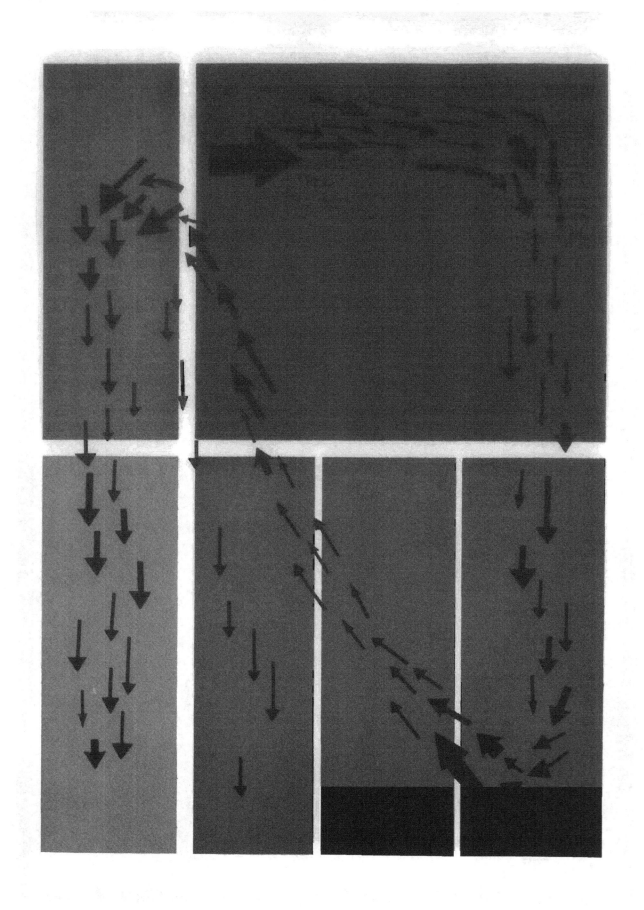

98

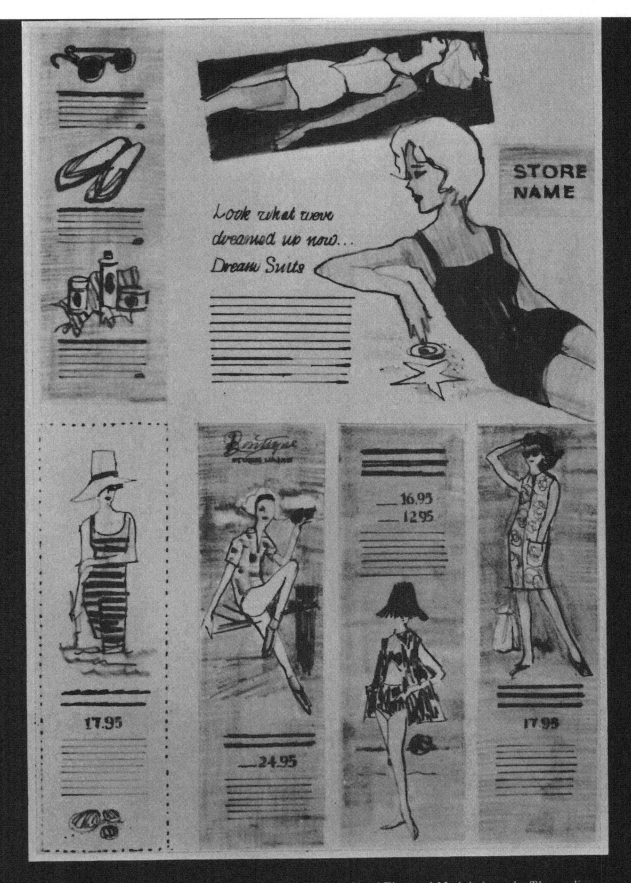

STORE
NAME

Look what we've
dreamed up now...
Dream Suits

17.95

24.95

16.95
12.95

17.95

*This layout like the one on page 97 is based on the combined Flow and Module formula. The application of the Module formula organizes the individual areas within the page. The Flow formula helps to create a dynamic, rather than a static arrangement of graphic elements within the individual areas.*

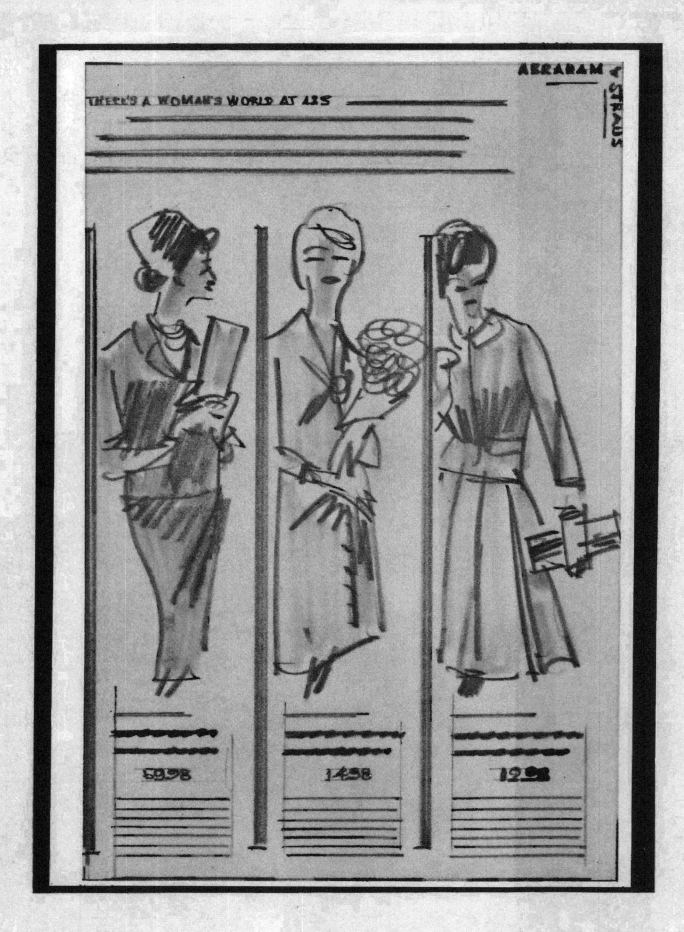

Here are 2 tabloid page omnibus layouts, based on the modular format. On the following pages are additional tabloid omnibus layouts, each also showing the modular format on which it is based.

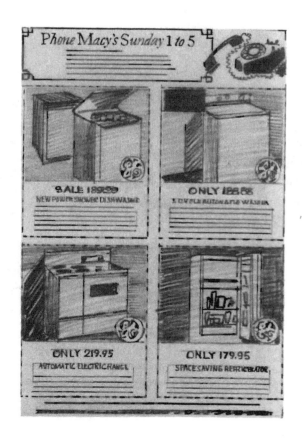

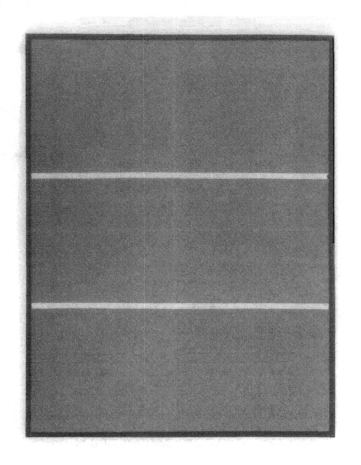

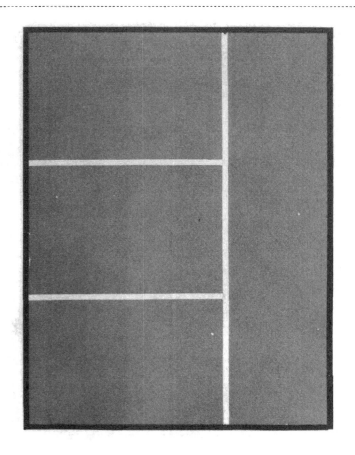

104

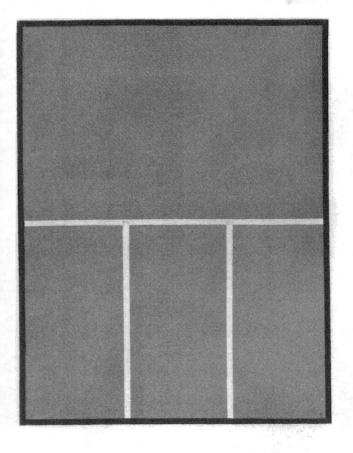

# LAYOUT—PART IV

## HOW TO CREATE AN ADVERTISING STYLE FOR A STORE

**AUTHOR'S NOTE:**

On April 5th, 1937 I started a new job as Art Director for L. Bamberger and Co., of Newark, New Jersey. The new Advertising Manager was George P. Slockbower, who started in that job on the same day. We were both invited to work for Bamberger's by the new Sales Promotion Director, Richard Weil Jr. We were the nucleus of a group that created a new kind of retail advertising.

IN MR. WEIL'S WORDS: *"In the first two years after its introduction (it) was the most widely copied store advertising style in America. It won every national advertising award worth winning . . . It received, in other words, considerable professional acclaim . . . The approbation indicated by the advertising awards was not in itself conclusive proof of anything. Nevertheless, in the absence of fixed measurements, it cannot but be reassuring to receive the critical approval of those expert practitioners in a professional field whose opinions presumably are the most worth having."*

Speaking for myself (and I'm sure that George Slockbower would concur) it was an exciting and rewarding business experience.

The first problem that faced us is the subject of this part of this chapter *How to Create an Advertising Style for a Store.* Richard Weil Jr. describes this project in Chapter 9 of his book "The Art of Practical Thinking," which was published in 1940 by Simon and Schuster.

The notes used by Mr. Weil for his book and my notes are obviously the same; all our meetings were carefully documented. Since his ability to analyze a problem and articulate the conclusions was one of his outstanding talents, I am taking the liberty of quoting some portions (including the quotes above) directly from his book and supplementing his material with my own, to emphasize the graphic objective of this book.

## A STORE ADVERTISING STYLE— PRO AND CON

*". . . we were going to start with the problem of the appearance of advertising, and the first question I wanted to explore, in the changing of the appearance of our own advertising, was the question of whether we should choose to create what is called in advertising circles, a store style. A store style is supposed to be a sufficiently consistent and individual method of handling the appearance of a store's advertising, so that at a glance, and even before a store's name is seen, it is apparent to the casual reader that the advertisement must be the product of that particular store and no other. The disadvantage of a store style might lie in two directions, monotony and inflexibility. The advantage in a store having a style is, first, individuality, for whatever that may be worth, and, second, whatever equity may inhere in the building up of an habitual recognition on the part of the reader of the store's offerings."*

There are two schools of thought about a store advertising style. One group recommends *The Policy of Consistency.* Every ad, they say, should reflect the spirit of every other ad—to help build one kind of image for a store. Another group recommends *The Policy of Innovation,* every ad different in style and different in character. This builds, they say, an image of drama and excitement for a store. Are the two schools of thought diametrically opposed? No! Either one or the other, or a combination of both, can be employed as a store advertising style.

### The paramount consideration is the need for a policy of planned continuity of graphic appearance

Obviously, the more advertising a store uses, the more opportunity the store has to develop both consistency and innovation and the easier it becomes to make the advertising style immediately recognizable to the reader. On the other hand, the less advertising a store uses, the harder the ads have to work to create a consistent store advertising style.

### Theoretical Requirements for a Store's Advertising Style

*". . . we came thus automatically to the questions of 'what style' and 'how to create it'. It seemed wise at this stage of the proceedings to construct a list of theoretical requirements to which any store style must conform in order to be acceptable. Accordingly we set about to construct this list . . . For any store style to be an acceptable one, it must meet the following requirements . . ."*

1. DIFFERENT—a store advertising style should be as different from your competition as your store is different.

2. BETTER—an advertising style should be better than the one you had before, and better than your competition's. Since better is a relative word, the decision as to what is better must be based on your own experience and judgment.

3. FLEXIBLE—a store style should allow a store to advertise any kind of merchandise at any time of the year and for both sale and non-sale events.

4. VIGOROUS—an advertising style should have vigor and vitality. This does not mean your advertising style should be black or buck-eye, but it does mean that it should not be wishy-washy.

5. SIMPLE—not complex. A store style should not draw attention to itself, but should help get the message read.

6. WITHIN REASON AS TO EXPENSE—obviously, a store advertising style that's based on a technique that a store can't afford, is not practical.

7. TEACHABLE TO OTHERS—if your rare genius leaves and takes his personal style with him, you're in trouble. The style must be one that is teachable to others.

8. LONG LIVED—a store style must be able to withstand the rigors of time and be able to change with the times, and still maintain its individual characteristics.

9. REPRODUCEABLE—newspapers have made great strides in engraving and printing, but even they have limitations. A store style should not be created with a graphic technique that *your* newspaper cannot reproduce. You'll both be disappointed.

10. REFLECT THE PERSONALITY OF THE STORE—an advertising style must reflect the character of the store. It must be consistent with the merchandise, the services, the appearance and the philosophy of the store.

### Factors which can be manipulated to produce a store style

*". . . It should be noted that no store is qualified, or should attempt to invent a new art form. The problem is strictly one of making out of old, recognized artistic elements a new synthesis which gains its individuality for the store simply by being a consistent combination of artistic ingredients not regularly used in that combination by competitive stores . . ."*

1. NEWSPAPER SPACE—
The way you use newspaper space—the consistency with which you use it, and shape of the space can be one of the first important factors in creating and maintaining a store style.

2. LAYOUT—
The arrangement and disposition of black and white areas is an important factor in creating the individuality required for a store style.

3. ART—
Whether you use drawing photographs or combinations of both, an inexhaustible variety of techniques are available to the designer.

## 4. TYPOGRAPHY—

There are over a thousand different type faces, and infinite combinations from which to choose. The consistent use of type faces helps to establish and maintain a store style.

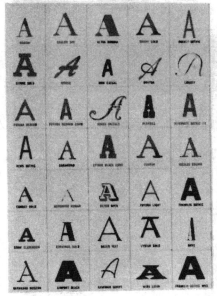

## 5. SIGNATURE CUT—

It is almost axiomatic that the first element to be changed when creating a store style is the signature art . . . Don't. It may not be the present signature cut that is wrong, it may be the way it is used that needs reviewing. However, if the signature cut is out of character with the new advertising style, then it might be wise to design a new one. A new signature cut alone is not enough to change the character of an advertising style.

## 6. PEOPLE—

They are among the most important factors in creating a store style. The proper job cannot be done without the right people . . . creative people with the leadership and the backing of top management.

## THE START . . . CREATING A GRAPHIC STORE STYLE

"*. . . Before we started in actually manipulating (the elements above) we did one rather useful trick. We laid out all the advertising of all our competitors for the past few weeks and listed those stylistic devices which all of them have in common. This list proved to be a valuable guide of things not to do. Whether the mannerisms they had in common were good or bad, we knew that if we wanted our style to be different, these were things to be avoided . . .*"

The graphic mannerisms of most stores' advertising are subtly different, in only a few cases radically different. Even with subtle differences a store can have a distinctive advertising style, provided the store uses these consistently. The illustrations on the next few pages (110-117) demonstrate the distinctive mannerisms used by some stores to give them the individuality they seek. For the purposes of direct comparison, the layouts were made in the same size and contain the same merchandise illustrations.

## THE THEORY BECOMES AN ACTUALITY

Of the six factors which can be manipulated to produce a store advertising style — newspaper space, layout, typography, art, signature cut, people—at Bamberger's we immediately chose the three most significant, which we felt were directly connected with the creativity of the graphic style.

"*. . . The first ingredient was layout. We adapted a layout principle involving the location of a sizable mass somewhere in the advertisement and a long curving sweep of merchandise issuing from the mass following the two sides of the outer boundary of the area being used.*

*The second ingredient was a choice of art technique. It seemed best to use a mixture of art techniques. We chose three: photography (or simulated photography such as wash drawings) for the large mass, line drawings for the sweep of merchandise away from the mass, and a sort of cross hatch technique typical of steel engravings for a general background for the line drawings of merchandise.*

*The third ingredient was a cinch, once we had made up our minds to avoid existing common practices so long as we could be better as well as different. It had long been a tradition in store advertising that the use of italics was to be avoided as you would the plague because of the lesser legibility of the italic type face. It had apparently been either forgotten or not known that earlier great printers had designed and used, with success, some few beautiful and legible italic faces. Accordingly, we adopted a classic Bodoni italic type face which assured us of the differences we were seeking . . . Now we had our store style.*"

The illustrations on pages 118 through 129 show the Bamberger store style from its initial stage through successive periods. The style was reviewed every six months for "*refreshment without loss of its original identity*" . . . . and once a year for a major innovation, to keep it from becoming sterile.

*Concertina pleats*
*twirl to the tune of Spring*

This is an incomplete layout showing three fashion figures, a hand lettered headline and a block of copy. It could be completed to reflect the
advertising style of any number of stores. What is the one vital graphic
device that makes it a Saks Fifth Avenue ad? See the opposite page.

Concertina pleats
twirl to the tune of Spring

The graphic device used by Saks Fifth Avenue is a distinctive border which includes the store's signature cut. Any arrangement of graphic elements used within this "magazine border" still says Saks Fifth Avenue and no other store.

Concertina pleats
twirl to the tune of Spring

This layout shows the same three dresses with a slight change in the color of the art, and a change of the headline treatment. It, too, could be completed to look like the advertising style of any number of stores. What simple graphic device makes it look like B. Altman & Co.? See opposite page.

The graphic device used by B. Altman & Co. is its distinctive signature cut
and its size and position in relation to the other elements of the ad. If a
store's signature has individuality and is used with graphic vigor, as
B. Altman & Co. does, then it can be used to establish a store's style.

This layout again shows the same three dresses in the same arrangement. Three graphic devices are used by Marshall Field & Co. to make their ads distinctive. What are they? See the opposite page.

*The three graphic devices used consistently by Marshall Field & Co. to make their advertising distinctive are as follows: (1) A hand lettered signature cut, always used at the top of the page and centered. (2) A horizontal block of copy across the top of the page and (3) A color variation in the art work.*

*Once again the same three dresses are used in the layout above, and again in relatively the same position. What graphic devices does Lord & Taylor use to make its advertising the most memorable in the country? See the next page.*

The three graphic devices used consistently by Lord & Taylor to make its advertising distinctively Lord & Taylor's are as follows: (1) A full and fluid wash drawing technique with the occasional use of contrasting free line drawings. (2) Integration of its line drawing signature into the loose wash background and ... (3) Short copy blocks of light face type accented by bold face.

The start of the style: a photographic mass, contrasting pen and ink art, a condensed type face (Onyx) for the headlines and Bodoni italic for the body type.

A variation of the style: this time the photographic mass is lower on the page, but all other factors are the same except the art. The art "flow" was a characteristic feature of the style that made it different from other stores' advertising.

## PLAY THE GAME OF LIVING STATUES WITH FALL FABRICS

*Alix of Paris, put women back on a pedestal with classic draperies, but the sculptural mode this Fall is a modified one, easier to wear and to make yourself. You'll carry out your design in BLACK, relieved with royal blue and red as Vionnet, or with grass green after Ardanse, and Schiaparelli reds. Greens are second best, especially dark blue tones and grayed shades, followed by wine-reds. Remember the big three Fall daytime colors—Black, Green and Wine. The daytime story is the old classic, smooth, drapeable fabrics which are favored by Alix, Heim and Paton. Flat crepes, Alpaca-weaves, Jerseys, Satins, Cantons and Jacquards and elabys, in pure silk, colamaus (acetate and rayon) and sheer wool. Priced from 1.98 to 4.95 a yard. With Mary Madison's Fabric Bureau to advise you and McCall Patterns with printed cutting lines it will be no trick at all to turn yourself into a fashion figurine in the 1937 manner.*

A. **PINNED IN**—the dark ... McCall Pattern No. 9 ... first executed in a smooth black body. The drape ... then used, dashed ... an brilliant colors at in silk ... yard, 1.98

B. **SOFT**—the gibbed bodice ... and draped shoulders is ... McCall Pattern No. 9 ... Sheer crepe in the crepe above sky, velvet or pure silk, in Lelong ... yard, 1.98

C. **SCULPTURED**—as the shell folds of the ladies and beautiful lines of the slanted sleeve featured in McCall Pattern No. 9155. Grass-wine is made of "Petit Pat", a pure silk canton velvet crepe, in the two blue greens of the nile ... yard, 1.98

D. **DECEIVING**—the folds of the bloused-casual exhibit racing varieties. McCall empire No. 9071 could be equally interesting in black rough fabrics, here or as preferred in silk, vogel satin pure silk, wine ... yard, 1.98

E. **TOP MYSTERY**—clearly must give the simple slant the best lines by repetitions over the Heim Empire McCall Pattern as as "Teresa" velvet sylvet, daytime repp in black blue ... yard, 1.98

F. **OUTLINE**—pearl like shirt and are throughout in McCall Pattern No. 9027 back, executed in "Tilamar" black jacquard crepe of acetate rayon, velvet or linen ... yard, 2.50

*The end of Phase One of the style: the purity of the style as shown here. was retained till a variation was designed and approved.*

Phase Three of the style: Two kinds of ads were developed, some with one figure, others with many. The graphic device used in every ad of this campaign was the cartouche. For more than six months these unusual borders became the trademark of every Bamberger ad.

Phase Four of the style: Unusual Texture . . . a variety of unusual textures were developed and used for complete backgrounds and for accents. In the ad on the opposite page, the texture was used as a decorative bull's-eye for a single fashion figure.

APPLAUSE

*Applause is the caviar and champagne of an actress's life. I'm sure the wonderful surge of acclaim that sweeps from boxes to balcony and back again at the end of a brilliant performance stirs her the thousandth time as deeply as the first.*

*At certain times we're all actresses. Entering a fashionable restaurant. Being ushered to a conspicuously good seat at the Ballet. Stepping out of a custom-built car. Those dramatic moments when we find ourselves suddenly spotlighted. Such moments make precious memories. Granted, we're not greeted with a thunder of audible applause, but the light in a gallant escort's eye, the wave of turned heads have the same intoxicating effect.*

BAMBERGER'S MINK COATS ARE $759 TO $3,500. FUR SALON, THIRD FLOOR

L. BAMBERGER & CO.

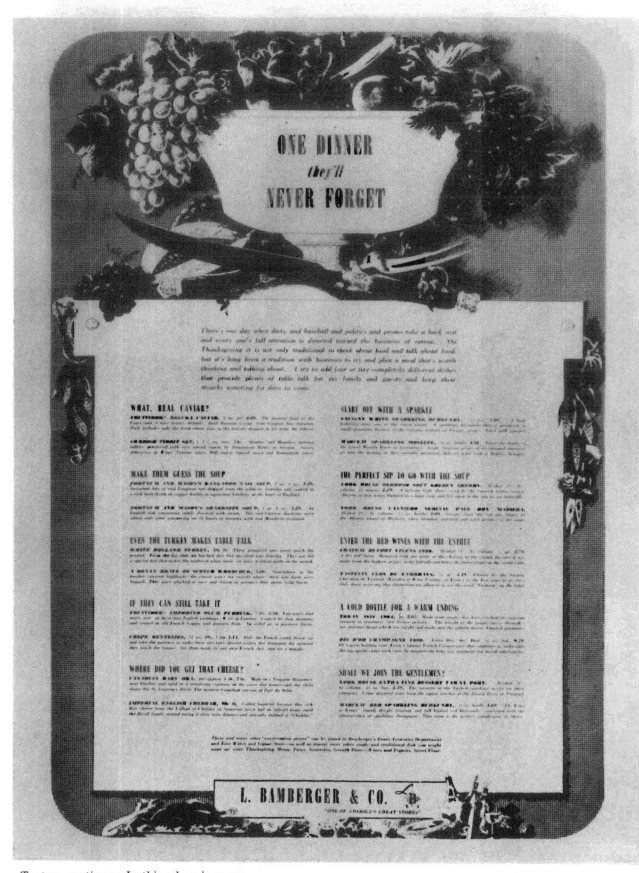

*Texture continues: In this ad, as in many others, the texture combined with the decorative pen and ink drawing was used to create a frame for the advertising message.*

*Texture plus Scale: An additional graphic innovation was added. We noticed that the illustrations in most ads, were about the same size. A change in scale could make an ad stand out from all others. The enlarged silhouette of the hand and arm was one of many devices used to achieve this objective.*

*Pen and Ink and Sweep: On many occasions we combined the best ingredients of previous campaigns for a new series. The merchandise in these two ads were so rich with their own texture and pattern, that we added little or no other graphic devices. The layout, however, had "sweep" and the art was the same pen and ink technique.*

# CHINTZ MAKES A ROOM
## *your very own*

You can tell more about a woman's character by spending one hour in her home than by days of cross-examination. For her home reflects her tastes and temperament more clearly than words. That's why, I think, so many women choose chintzes to create a congenial background. That's why, too, so many women choose them from a special collection here in New Jersey. For these chintzes with their warm and lovely colors, their wealth of patterns, give a woman leeway to choose exactly the kind of charm she wants her room to radiate.

There are prim, precise patterns in the Early American manner, great sweeping florals in the most formal country-house tradition, ribbons-and-laces for Victorians, plaids and stripes for Moderns. And though for years we've looked to England for our supply, American printers today are making chintzes every bit as lovely, far less expensive, and with the added virtue of being washable. All of which makes decorating a simple and extremely satisfying matter.

**AN UNUSUAL COLLECTION OF WASHABLE CHINTZES EXCLUSIVE WITH BAMBERGER'S IN NEWARK**

*For upholstery, slip-covers, draperies, dressing-table skirts, bedspreads, features 18 patterns in Colonial, Victorian and Modern designs, in a wide range of colors. All are resistant to sunlight. All are 36" wide. From 79c to 1.00 yard.*

BAMBERGER'S UPHOLSTERY, SIXTH FLOOR

## L. BAMBERGER & CO.
"ONE OF AMERICA'S GREAT STORES"

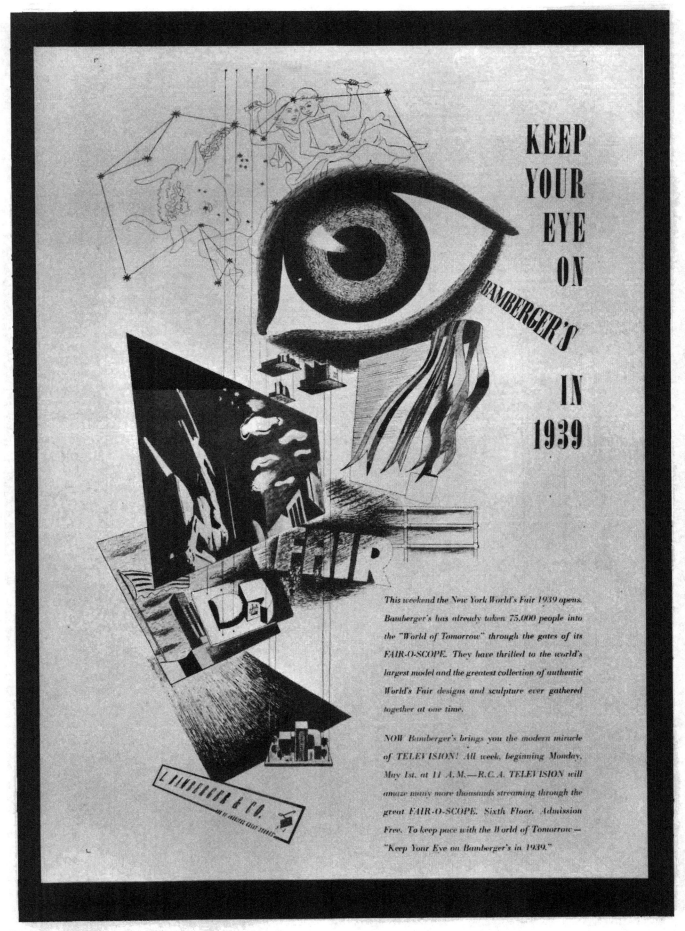

# KEEP YOUR EYE ON BAMBERGER'S IN 1939

This weekend the New York World's Fair 1939 opens. Bamberger's has already taken 75,000 people into the "World of Tomorrow" through the gates of its FAIR-O-SCOPE. They have thrilled to the world's largest model and the greatest collection of authentic World's Fair designs and sculpture ever gathered together at one time.

NOW Bamberger's brings you the modern miracle of TELEVISION! All week, beginning Monday, May 1st, at 11 A.M.—R.C.A. TELEVISION will amaze many more thousands streaming through the great FAIR-O-SCOPE. Sixth Floor. Admission Free. To keep pace with the World of Tomorrow—"Keep Your Eye on Bamberger's in 1939."

*Dimension: The most difficult graphic technique to achieve; to convey a feeling of depth on a flat printed surface. Here are two examples of a series that ran for six months*

**Everything is the same...but different.** In 1960 Macy's introduced a new idea in home furnishings called Palazzo. It is a vast correlated group for every room in the house, based on the styles of the English Regency and Italian Ottocento. Stores all over the country were invited to participate in this merchandise promotion. For their guidance, Macy's prepared a sales promotion kit, complete with artwork, logos, copy, layouts, posters, commercials, display and window ideas, publicity releases. On the next pages you will see how 7 of these stores told their customers about Palazzo. All the elements were the same, because all the stores drew on the contents of the sales promotion kit. Yet each ad is different, each ad is as individual as the store advertising Palazzo. Why? Because every store has taken these elements and interpreted them so they reflect the style of the specific store.

# THERE'S A NEW WORD
# PALAZZO
# A NEW FASHION FOR YOUR HOME

**What is Palazzo?**

Palazzo is many things . . . all of them beautiful. It's a fashion so new, yet so classic, a fashion that until now you could only find in antiques and expensive decorator shops. It's a huge and varied and beautiful group of furniture and accessories, all reflecting the elegance of the English Regency and the Italian Ottocento.

**How did Palazzo start?**

It began two years ago with an idea of Macy's, a conviction that you wanted greater elegance in your home. We took it from there and spent two years in research, two years in which our designers worked with artists and other designers and manufacturers all over the world to create Palazzo.

**What does Palazzo include?**

There are tables and tablecloths, beds and sheets, curtains and silverware, sofas and towels, rugs and lamps . . . just about everything for every room in your home except the kitchen. You can furnish or refurnish a whole house with Palazzo, down to the last ash tray . . . but even if all you want is a new lamp, you'll want a Palazzo lamp, because Palazzo is so lovely.

**Why is Palazzo different?**

Palazzo is not a pattern but a theme. The scroll on a delicate tambour curtain and a thickly textured rug are not the same . . . but related. The pattern on a crystal goblet has a family resemblance to the border on a pillow case . . . but it's not identical. This is coordination so subtle that it results not in sameness but in beauty.

**Are there Palazzo colors?**

Yes, but Palazzo is not a color; it's a spectrum. There's lots of gold and black and white . . . and also soft violets, rich corals, warm greens, many shades of many colors. Macy's carried each color swatch thousands of miles to make sure that everything that is Palazzo would go together.

**Who makes Palazzo?**

Some of the country's top makers worked with Macy's in creating and coordinating Palazzo . . . names you're proud to own, like Drexel, Gorham, Cabin Crafts. And Palazzo also includes enchanting imports from Italy, Switzerland, and the Far East. Everything that is Palazzo is superbly made . . . and looks far more costly than it is.

**What does Palazzo look like?**

Come to Macy's tomorrow and see for yourself. See Palazzo in all our 76 windows: living rooms, bedrooms, dining rooms and all the lovely accessories that go with them. Then see the Palazzo Pavilion on Macy's 7th floor and Palazzo on Macy's street, 6th, 7th, 8th and 9th floors at Herald Square or at the Macy branch store in your neighborhood. For Palazzo is all around you at Macy's now.

# TOMORROW AT MACY'S
# BE SURROUNDED BY THE NEW
# ELEGANCE THAT IS PALAZZO

# here comes

## Palazzo

...sweeping in on a great wave of excitement. A new word. A new idea. A new fashion for your home. It's Palazzo! A look of ageless elegance, rich simplicity and classic beauty—borrowed from the best of the English Regency and Italian 18th Century. See Palazzo furniture, rich and mellow fruitwood. See Palazzo fabrics...from Swiss Tambour muslins to Italian silk damask.

Palazzo floor coverings...Palazzo silverware. Palazzo china and deep-cut crystal...accessories everywhere! One word, one look—it's Palazzo! Only at... MEIER & FRANK'S a place for everything.

DOWNTOWN · LLOYD'S · SALEM

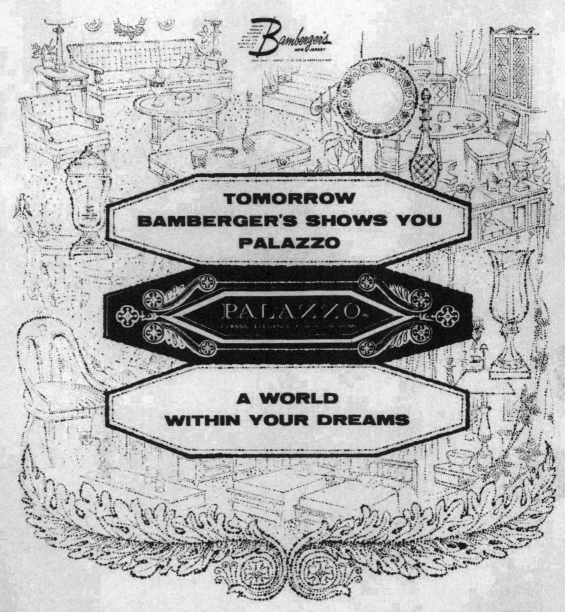

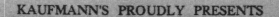

134

# PALAZZO

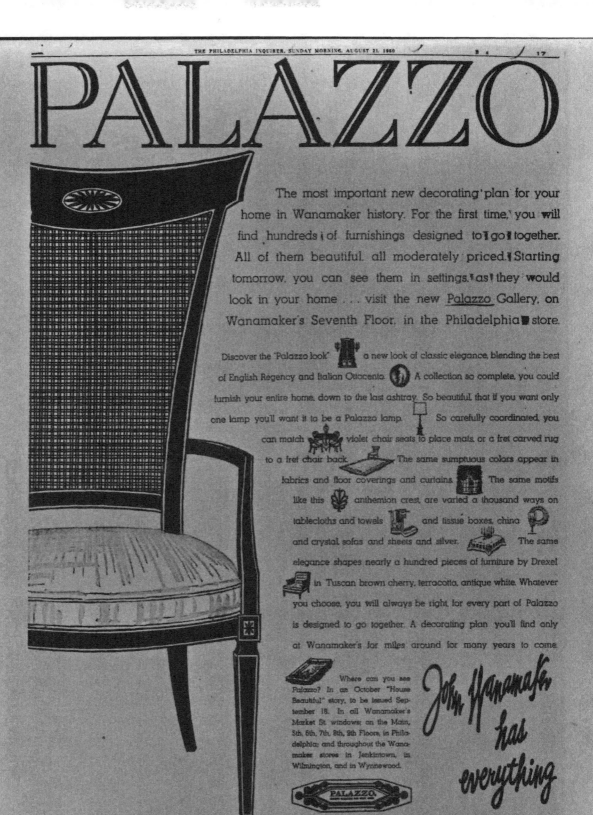

The most important new decorating plan for your home in Wanamaker history. For the first time, you will find hundreds of furnishings designed to go together. All of them beautiful, all moderately priced. Starting tomorrow, you can see them in settings, as they would look in your home . . . visit the new Palazzo Gallery, on Wanamaker's Seventh Floor, in the Philadelphia store.

Discover the "Palazzo look" a new look of classic elegance, blending the best of English Regency and Italian Ottocento. A collection so complete, you could furnish your entire home, down to the last ashtray. So beautiful, that if you want only one lamp you'll want it to be a Palazzo lamp. So carefully coordinated, you can match violet chair seats to place mats, or a fret carved rug to a fret chair back. The same sumptuous colors appear in fabrics and floor coverings and curtains. The same motifs like this anthemion crest, are varied a thousand ways on tablecloths and towels and tissue boxes, china and crystal, sofas and sheets and silver. The same elegance shapes nearly a hundred pieces of furniture by Drexel in Tuscan brown cherry, terracotta, antique white. Whatever you choose, you will always be right, for every part of Palazzo is designed to go together. A decorating plan you'll find only at Wanamaker's for miles around for many years to come.

Where can you see Palazzo? In an October "House Beautiful" story, to be issued September 18. In all Wanamaker's Market St. windows; on the Main, 5th, 6th, 7th, 8th, 9th Floors, in Philadelphia; and throughout the Wanamaker stores in Jenkintown, in Wilmington, and in Wynnewood.

PALAZZO

*John Wanamaker has everything*

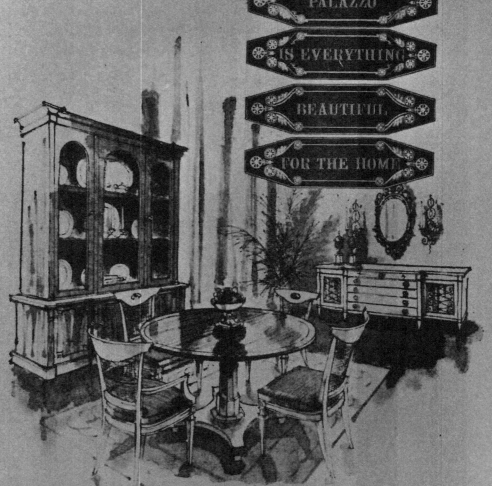

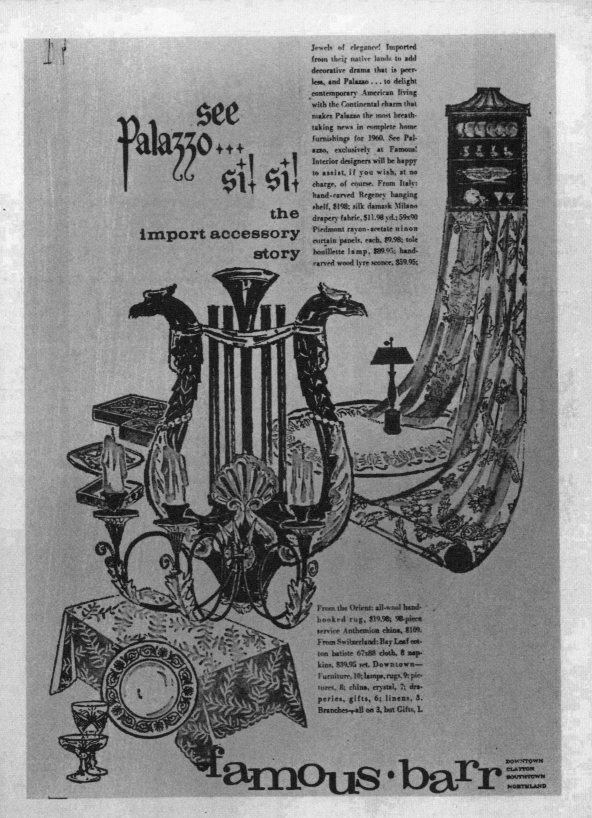

# LAYOUT—PART V

## HOW TO DESIGN A CAMPAIGN

### EVERY AD IS PART OF A CAMPAIGN

Once a store advertising style is established and every ad bears the same family resemblance, a store campaign has been established. From time to time, however, a store finds it necessary to create a group of ads to satisfy a particular promotional need. These ads are taken out of context and are labeled "a campaign."

Stores do this primarily for additional emphasis on:

1. Special events.
2. Special merchandise classifications.
3. Division or department emphasis.
4. Special seasons (like Christmas).
5. Store services, etc.

The variety and number of campaigns that a store runs depends on the store's advertising objectives. Many stores divide all their advertising into major campaigns, for women's fashion, for homefurnishings, for men, etc.

This can lead to three or four store styles rather than one. Are the individual parts more important than the whole? Or is the whole more important than the sum of all of its parts? This question, too, must be resolved by the individual store and the objectives of the store's sales promotion policy. A store that runs a heavy newspaper advertising schedule can afford a number of satellite campaigns without destroying its over-all store style. Actually, as a matter of good advertising practice, such stores should run a variety of meaningful campaigns to add excitement and dramatize important segments of the store's image.

### "#1 OF A SERIES"

The line "#1 of a Series" is often used at the top of an ad by many stores to emphasize the fact that this ad is a part of a campaign. In itself it does not excite the reader nor does it make an ad part of a recognizable campaign. This statement is a self-satisfying one and is more like talking to yourself. If a campaign needs this statement, to hold it together, review the elements—some important ingredient is missing.

These are some of the ingredients required to make a good campaign—use them all and then if you wish, add "#1 of a Series". . .

### 1. Frequency of Appearance

The more concentrated the advertising schedule, the more effective the campaign.

### 2. Similarity of Ad Size and Shape

An advertising campaign can use small ads or large ads, but consistency of size and shape will create a more memorable impression.

### 3. Recognizable Graphic Appearance

A. *Layout*—as many layout factors as possible should be used consistently and with enough creative courage so that the ads do not become monotonous.

B. *Art*—use an art style that's immediately recognizable as being different—or a method of utilizing the conventional art forms that make it appear to be different—but above all, use the technique consistently throughout the campaign.

C. *Type*—the same type face or type faces should be used throughout the campaign—again for consistency.

D. *Symbols*—the inclusion of a symbol in itself does not make the campaign more recognizable unless the symbol is used with consistency and as a positive element in the campaign.

While most ads in a campaign should be as consistently alike as "peas in a pod," there are occasions when it's good sales promotion judgment to make each ad in a campaign as different from the other as you can.

This is possible only when the ads are impressive graphically and are run in large space units in the paper.

The illustrations on the next few pages show some of the campaigns used by Macy's New York—some as alike as "peas in a pod," some as different as they could be made.

*The furniture ads shown on the opposite page and on the two pages that follow represent an ideal campaign. These ads contain every essential ingredient necessary to a campaign. The ads appeared in the same newspaper and on the same page of the newspaper at least once a month for almost three years. They were always designed in the same ad size and shape, always with the same layout formula, always the same art technique, and always the same typography and typographic arrangement. The campaign required no symbol for additional continuity because the ad itself was a symbol in its purest graphic form.*

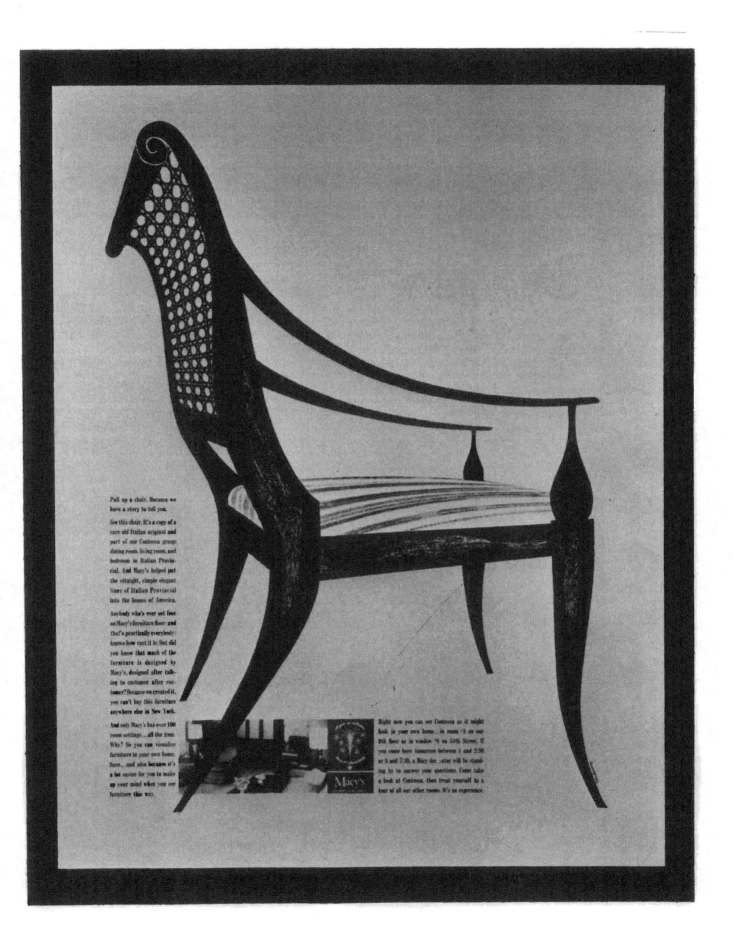

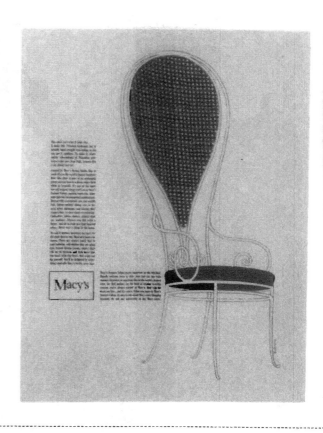

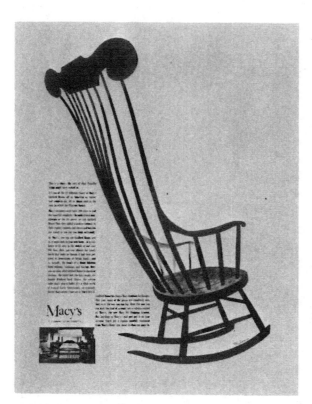

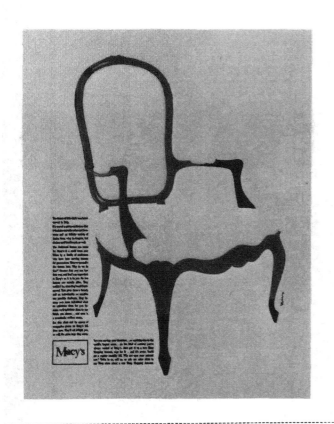

*The world is so full of a number of thing*

**Macy's has MORE of just about everything**

# The world is so full of a number of things

# Macy's has MORE of just about everything

# MACY'S ANNUAL GALA FOR ALL NEW YORK
# FIREWORKS
## ON THE HUDSON

 **WEDNESDAY, JUNE 29 AT 9 P.M.**

**FIREWORKS** MACY'S THRILLING TRADITIONAL INDEPENDENCE DAY TREAT **FIREWORKS**
A PYROTECHNIC EXTRAVAGANZA THAT WILL LIGHT UP THE SKY

A JOYOUS JUBILEE TO CELEBRATE OUR

NEW FLAG WITH ITS 50 SHINING STARS

**SPELLBINDING**
**SYMPHONY**
**OF BLAZING**
**BOMBARDMENTS**

MACY'S INVITES ALL TO OUR DARING DISPLAY

NATIVE OR STRANGER, URBAN, OR SUBURBAN

**FIREWORKS** (vertical, left) **FIREWORKS** (vertical, right)

## FROM MACY'S FOR THE WHOLE CITY TO ENJOY...FIREWORKS ON THE HUDSON RIVER...WEDNESDAY, JUNE 29... 9 P.M.

THE WORLD'S LARGEST AND MOST EXCITING STORE MACY'S

# FIREWORKS

!!!! THIS YEAR !!!!
STUPENDOUS SALUTE IN HONOR OF THE COMING 1960 ELECTIONS
—GLAD GREETINGS TO 550 VISITORS:—
THE BRITISH TOURNAMENT AND TATTOO
EVERY YEAR: SENSATIONAL STAR OF THE N.Y. SUMMER FESTIVAL

On the Hudson River from 2nd Street to 125th Street
NEW JERSEY
Hudson River
NEW YORK
Watch it from the New York side, from the Jersey side

## IN CASE OF RAIN

Macy's fireworks on the Hudson River will be held over till the next night: Thursday, June 30. Same place, same time, same constant cacophony of delightful detonations

## COME ONE, COME ALL...SEE MACY'S FASCINATING FANTASY OF FIREWORKS ON THE HUDSON RIVER

# PARADE

# THURSDAY AT 9:45 AM

## MORE COLOSSAL, MORE CAPTIVATING, MORE COLORFUL THAN EVER

SEE BOBBY CLARK ON THE GOOD SHIP EMILY MORGAN

TA-RA-RA-RA CONNIE FRANCIS AS CINDERELLA TA-RA-RA-RA

MERRY CHRISTMAS MUSIC ALL THE WAY

SEE SHIRLEY TEMPLE AND HER CHILDREN

### CELEBRITIES

**LINE OF MARCH**

**SHIRLEY TEMPLE**
She'll be here with her three children . . . Lori, Charles Jr., and Susan. See them on the Story Book Queen float.

**CHUCK CONNORS**
"The Rifleman" of ABC TV will be riding along cowboy style. Look for him on his trusty horse.

**DOLORES GRAY**
She's from the musical hit "Destry Rides Again." Watch for her as she rides by on her favorite pony.

**36 ROCKETTES**
Radio City's famous Music Hall Rockettes will be on the transparent gift box float. Story'll be seeing all you.

**PAT CARROLL**
The star of ABC TV's "Keep Talking" will be Mother Goose on the first of the nursery rhyme floats.

**CONNIE FRANCIS**
MGM Records' singing star will be our beautiful Cinderella. See her on the pumpkin coach.

**JULES MUNSHIN**
Star of the Broadway stage and television, he'll be Old King Cole on his own merry float.

**N.Y. CITY CENTER LIGHT OPERA CO.**
The famous New York singing company will be riding in the Carousel float. Hear them.

**BOBBY CLARK**
The beloved comedian of the American stage will be Captain Macy on the good ship Emile Morgan. Say hello as he sails by.

**ED WYNN**
This delightful star will greet Santa Claus.

**AND SANTA CLAUS**
Star of every Macy Thanksgiving Day Parade.

## FABULOUS FANTASTIC
## FLEET OF FLOATS
## TOWERING BALLOONS
## BEVIES OF BEAUTIFUL MARCHERS

### GIANT BALLOONS

DOLORES GRAY CHUCK CONNORS AND THEIR HOSSES

SEE AND HEAR CITY CENTER CHORISTERS

## CAVALCADE OF
## COMICAL CLOWNS
## HORDES OF INDIANS ON HORSEBACK
## BANDS, BANDS, & MORE BANDS

SKATERS DRUM MAJORETTES STUNTS

36 BEAUTIFUL ROCKETTES 36

### WHERE & WHEN

9:48 77TH ST.
CENTRAL PARK
10:12 COLUMBUS CIRCLE
10:40 TIMES SQUARE
34TH ST.
11:00 MACY'S

## RAIN OR SHINE ✸ COME ONE, COME ALL TO MACY'S THANKSGIVING DAY PARADE

*A formal layout: The strong, illustrative photographic focal point helped to get this Own Brand ad seen and read.*

*A traditional layout: An interesting headline, and an illustration of children in an unusual pose, was all that was necessary to get this Own Brand ad read.*

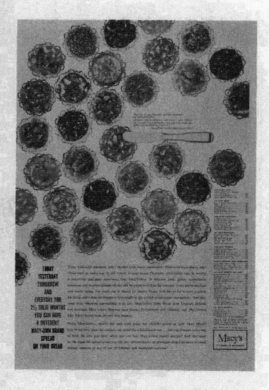

*A layout with exciting pattern: This is an ad selling Own Brand jellies and jams. How much more exciting it is for the reader to see the shimmering product rather than the static jars and labels.*

*A layout with an unusual focal point: The objective of this ad was to sell Own Brand paint to women. The old engraving of a very feminine woman in a paint ad was a provocative contradiction.*

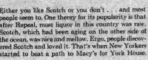

Either you like Scotch or you don't . . . and most people seem to. One theory for its popularity is that after Repeal, most liquor in this country was raw. Scotch, which had been aging on the other side of the ocean, was nice and mellow. Ergo, people discovered Scotch and loved it. That's when New Yorkers started to beat a path to Macy's for York House.

Today we drink everything from anisette to zubrovka. Scotch, however, is not only holding its own but is on the increase (sevenfold since 1935). Yet, even though more people are drinking more kinds of Scotch, Macy's-Own York House outsells all other 54 brands combined at Macy's by 3 to 1. There must be a reason.

Scotch drinking is not new. Clansmen were downing it in the 15th and 16th centuries. But any resemblance between what they drank and York House is only in the name . . . whisky. (From usquebaugh which is Gaelic for aqua vitae which is Latin for water of life.)

How does one Scotch differ from the next? In flavor. Most current Scotches are blends of highland malts and grain whiskies. (The straight malt Scotch is an acquired taste, unless you were born to the bagpipes.) York House is a judicious blend that appeals to almost all; light, but with character so you know you're drinking Scotch.

You hear a lot of chat about Highland water, peat, and the sherry casks used to age Scotch. They're important, but the blending is more important. Most important of all is consistency. The Scotch you drink today should taste like the Scotch you drank last year. York House always does. For generations, York House has been made in the same place by the same people to the same formula.

The spirit of Dr. Cowie is bottled in every fifth of York House. Who was he? The man who made Scotches for Macy's at the turn of the century and whose exceptional standards and unerring skill are faithfully followed today.

Macy's Taster, who goes far enough back to have actually met Dr. Cowie, and whose palate has been unchallenged for over 50 years, says "Quality for quality, you can't buy a better Scotch for the money than York House." So why pay more . . . when you can buy York House?

If you're a York House drinker, skip this paragraph. It's for those of the younger generation who may possibly never have tasted York House. They weren't even born when the York House tradition began. To them we say just this: buy one bottle of York House and compare it to the Scotch you're now drinking. That's all. You'll understand why so many New Yorkers will drink nothing else . . . and would do so, even if York House weren't such a wonderful buy.

There's one interesting fact about York House. You can buy it in only one place in New York . . . Macy's. Yet, despite this, York House is the drink served in thousands and thousands of homes. It's a lot easier to buy other Scotches . . . but they're not Macy's York House. It's as simple as all that.

Macy's-Own Brands are a tradition in New York . . . for their consistently high quality and consistently low prices. Of all, York House Scotch is probably the best known. We suspect there are even people drinking it who don't realize York House is Macy's-Own, but just the brand of Scotch they prefer. We don't mind, except that we're so very proud of it.

# MACY'S-OWN BRAND YORK HOUSE SCOTCH

86.8 proof. 4 5 quart, **5.99**; 3 for **17.43**. Case of 12, **68.29**.

York House Special Reserve Scotch. The same distinguished flavor, but older than regular York House. 86.8 proof. 4 5 quart, **7.19**; 3 for **20.92**. Case of 12, **81.97**.

York House Signature Scotch. Limited quantity only, from a remarkable, specially aged reserve. 86.8 proof. 4 5 quart, **8.79**; 3 for **25.58**. Case of 12, **98.98**.

Come, write, phone LA 4-3600. Macy's Fine Wine & Liquor Store, 459 Seventh Ave., La 1, 1. State. Fed. taxes included. In N. Y. C., add 3% sales tax. Deliveries only within N. Y. State (outside our regular delivery area, prepaid orders only, express charges collect).

(A) "Symbols—The inclusion of a symbol in itself does not make the campaign more recognizable unless the symbol is used with consistency and as a positive element in the campaign. . . ."

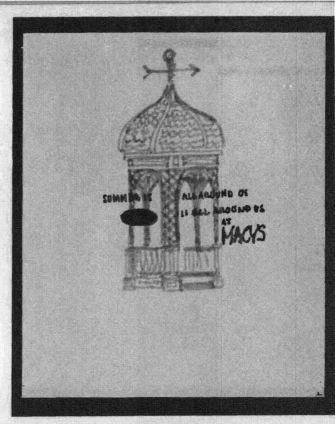

(B) The doodles shown on these two pages represent a few of many sketches made in the search for a proper symbol for an extensive campaign.

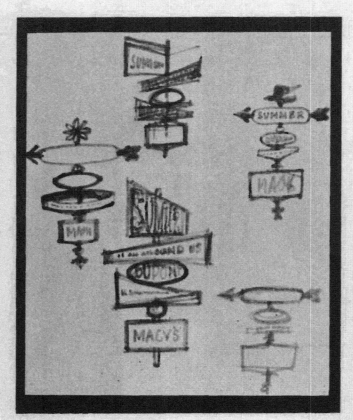

(E) The sketches shown here were in the right direction but still too complex.

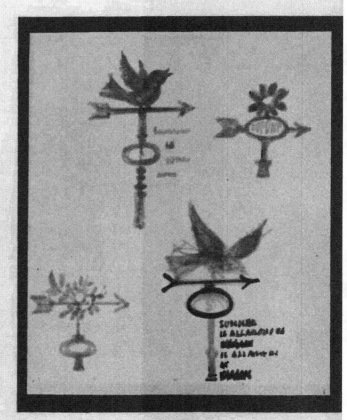

(F) These sketches show an attempt to simplify, but in doing so, the copy became an additional element too difficult to control in the ads.

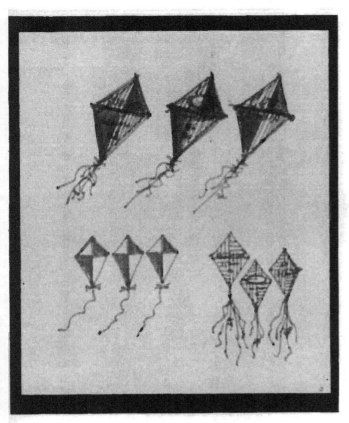

(C) A proper symbol should help tell the story, should have good silhouette, should be practical for small space as well as large and, above all, should be distinctive.

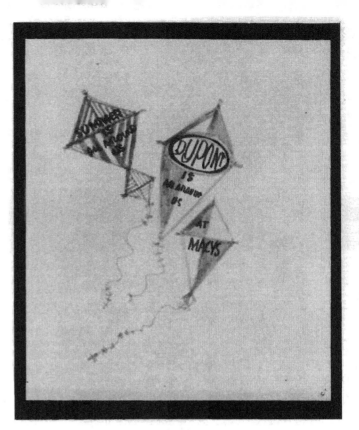

(D) On the next two pages you will see how the final symbol was used to help identify the ads as a campaign.

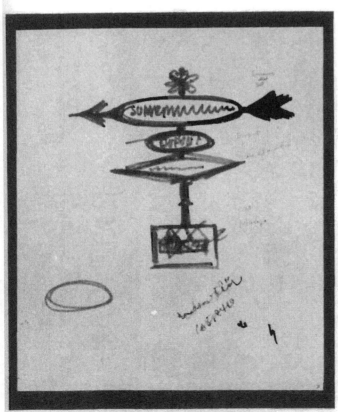

(G) Here the decision was made; that the symbol must include the entire copy story.

(H) The end of the doodle ... the search for an idea was ended ... the final design could now be drawn—see the next 2 pages for the final symbol and how it was used.

*Note the symbol and its use with men's merchandise. The symbol had to lend itself to all kinds of merchandise.*

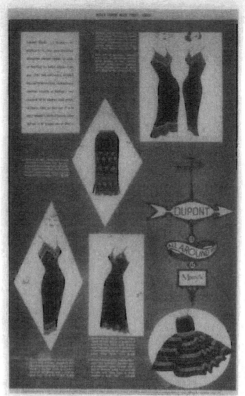

*The campaign consisted of light as well as dark background ads—the symbol was designed for both—its silhouette had to be clearly defined.*

*The symbol was used with variations of copy and size. Here it is used as part of the signature in the ad.*

*Note that this ad looks like the Men's ad above with the symbol used in the same way. This, then, becomes a campaign within a campaign.*

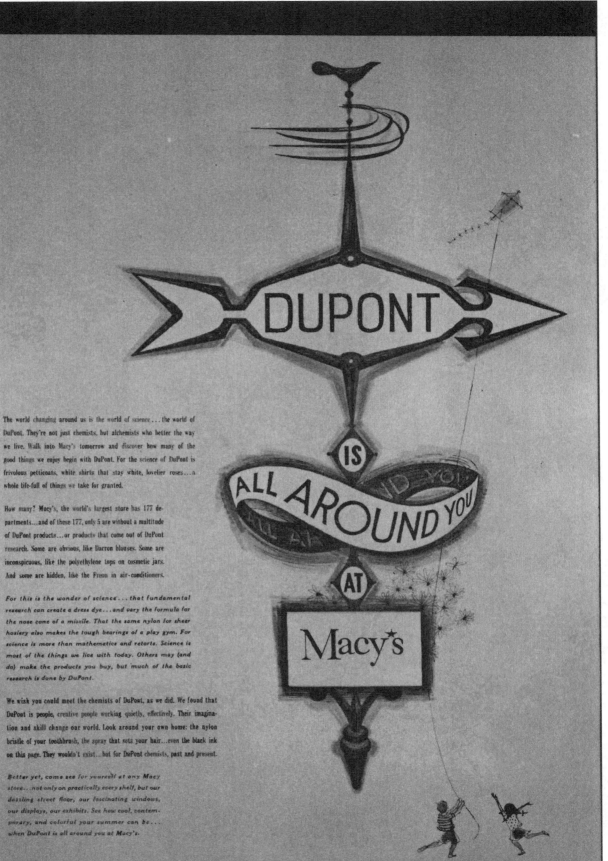

The world changing around us is the world of science... the world of DuPont. They're not just chemists, but alchemists who better the way we live. Walk into Macy's tomorrow and discover how many of the good things we enjoy begin with DuPont. For the science of DuPont is frivolous petticoats, white shirts that stay white, lovelier roses...a whole life-full of things we take for granted.

How many? Macy's, the world's largest store has 177 departments...and of these 177, only 5 are without a multitude of DuPont products...or products that come out of DuPont research. Some are obvious, like Dacron blouses. Some are inconspicuous, like the polyethylene tops on cosmetic jars. And some are hidden, like the Freon in air-conditioners.

*For this is the wonder of science... that fundamental research can create a dress dye...and vary the formula for the nose cone of a missile. That the same nylon for sheer hosiery also makes the tough bearings of a play gym. For science is more than mathematics and retorts. Science is most of the things we live with today. Others may (and do) make the products you buy, but much of the basic research is done by DuPont.*

We wish you could meet the chemists of DuPont, as we did. We found that DuPont is people, creative people working quietly, effectively. Their imagination and skill change our world. Look around your own home: the nylon bristle of your toothbrush, the spray that sets your hair...even the black ink on this page. They wouldn't exist...but for DuPont chemists, past and present.

*Better yet, come see for yourself at any Macy store...not only on practically every shelf, but our dazzling street floor, our fascinating windows, our displays, our exhibits. See how cool, contemporary, and colorful your summer can be... when DuPont is all around you at Macy's.*

*The final symbol design dominating a full page ad and helped to identify all future ads in the campaign.*

# FOR GENTLEMEN OF FASHION AND THEIR LADIES

**Gentlemen: we shall be frank.** Macy's Men's store has long been an exciting, intriguing, but frustrating place to shop. Not that we didn't have what you wanted, but it often took the lion-hearted to track it down. That's all changed now. Raymond Loewy has redesigned the Men's Store for us, opened up the aisles so you can browse, put everything where you can see it, and even tripled the candle-power overhead. It's a complete transformation, because when Macy's does something, we do it proud. Here are the monumental assortments that have always made Macy's Men's Store unique, assortments so vast they include the exceptional (16 kinds of detachable collars) as well as the expected (121 different styles of suspenders). Here are the bountiful imports...the English Argyles, the Italian sweaters, the French gloves...fine furnishings from all over the world so characteristic of Macy's. Here are classics, like striped repps; the news, like pocket foulards; the names, like Schiatti of Italy. Because whether you're conservative or a fashion pioneer, Macy's knows what men of good taste want...and has it. And, being Macy's, we have it in quantity. Not just a row of shirts, but 328 feet of shirts...longer than the flight of a home run in Yankee Stadium. Not just a shelf of sweaters, but a wall full. All in a home so new even elevator facades and entrances have been changed. But come see it for yourself tomorrow: Macy's Men's Store in all its new magnificence.

**Footnote for the ladies...** who shop so often in Macy's Men's Store. For all its new magnificence, you'll be glad to know many things remain unchanged. Like Macy's thrifty prices. You can buy socks here for 69c or 4.69...and they're both good buys. Like Macy's assortments...more of about everything you can imagine. Like expert advice...from our score of shirt salesmen, with an astounding average of 25.2 years at Macy's. From a mere shred of description, they find just the right shirt for your husband. Like our high standards, important to you because you're always concerned with the way things act after they've been bought. Washables wash, cleanables clean, and everything wears the way you expect it to. And what we've added or changed in Macy's Men's Store, you'll like. The bigger gift shop, the wider aisles, the sumptuous settings, the fact that most things are where you can see them. You've always shopped here with confidence. Now you'll enjoy shopping here even more.

## 34th STREET · 7th AVENUE · STREET FLOOR

Cuff links to give, cuff links to own, cuff links from the whole wide world. Now Macy's brings you Swank's Arts of the World cuff links, an entirely original and stunning collection. Each was carefully created and chosen for the great characteristics and skills of the distant land it represents. Denmark? Find hand-painted Royal Copenhagen porcelain. Spain? Enjoy Damascene inlaid with 24 Karat gold. England? Royal Scots Guards buttons. Holland? Delft tiles. And more, many more, all equally distinguished. These range from 3.50 to $20, so we've cuff links for everyone, everywhere, a consideration typical of Macy's. Now come, select yours, the collection is installed for you in Macy's magnificent new Men's Store, on the Street Floor at Herald Square.

## MACY'S NEW 🦁 MEN'S STORE

*The double truck ad on the preceding two pages was the start of a new campaign...Its objective: to make each ad as strikingly dramatic as possible. This campaign was scheduled to run in as concentrated a time as practical for greater reader impact. One consistent element was the identifying lion.*

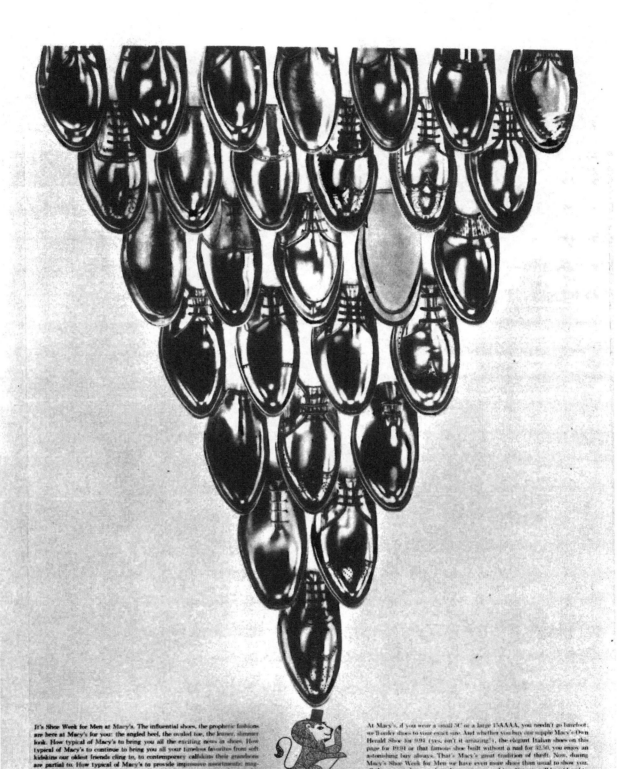

It's Shoe Week for Men at Macy's. The influential shoes, the prophetic fashions are here at Macy's for you: the angled heel, the ovaled toe, the leaner, slimmer look. How typical of Macy's to bring you all the exciting news in shoes. How typical of Macy's to continue to bring you all your timeless favorites from soft kidskins our oldest friends cling to, to contemporary calfskins their grandsons are partial to. How typical of Macy's to provide impressive assortments: magnificent Macy-Own Brands, splendid English imports, enormously popular made-in-Italy shoes, comfortable casuals that set New York men on their toes. How typical of Macy's to bring you hearty variety to your individual dimensions.

At Macy's, if you wear a small 5C or a large 15AAAA, you needn't go barefoot; we'll order shoes to your exact size. And whether you buy our supple Macy's-Own Herald Shoe for 9.91 (yes, isn't it amazing!), the elegant Italian shoes on this page for 19.91 or that famous shoe built without a nail for 32.50, you enjoy an astonishing buy always. That's Macy's great tradition of thrift. Now, during Macy's Shoe Week for Men we have even more shoes than usual to show you, all the newest shoes are here for you to see and try. Experts will be on hand to help you find the shoes that fit you best. Come to our Men's Shoe Store, 2nd floor, by way of our magnificent new Men's Store, 7th Avenue at 34th Street.

**IT'S SHOE WEEK FOR MEN AT MACY'S, AND BE SURE TO SEE MACY'S NEW MEN'S STORE, IT'S OPEN NOW**

The campaign continues . . . this time with an ad that's designed to relate the Men's Store to another campaign. Its design characteristic: a large light drawing made to look even bigger by placing the copy as low as possible on the page.

The large photographic illustration in this ad is used as a startling change of pace from the large light illustration on the left.

Another innovation, the editorial format, with equal emphasis on art and copy. Notice, however, the emphasis on the "Lion" symbol which helps identify the ad as part of the campaign.

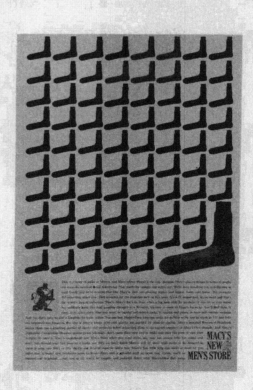

A repeat pattern of a single item creates visual drama. The symbol again helps to identify the ad as part of the campaign.

# MACY'S NEW MEN'S STORE CELEBRATES THE GREAT TRADITION OF ENGLISH FASHIONS FOR MEN

**Dashing!**
The tailored suit. You might very well have ordered it on Savile Row, our fine British worsteds in a suit carefully cut to your measure. You'll find your jacket slightly shorter, your waistline suppressed. The breast pocket is gone, trousers are uncuffed and pleatless, and the extension waistband narrowed. Happily, you've only to order it in our Merchant Tailoring Shop, 99.50.

**Righto!**
Cashmere-lined gloves. The fine glove; a tribute to British skill. Warm as a friendly handshake . . . carefully hand-sewn . . . hand-detailed capeskin. An exercise in superior workmanship. 9.98

**Quite!**
*The cardigan. Here we have the incomparable cardigan in the great sweater tradition. As British as Trafalgar Square, with its fine woolen yarn, lightweight bulk and pleasant welcome warmth. 32.94*

**Posh!**
*Macy's-Own Saybrooke dress shirt. The finest English combed cotton broadcloth went into Macy's-Own Saybrooke, that's Macy's tradition. The result is a dress shirt so luxurious it is quite like silk to the touch, actually feels smoother after repeated wear. And Macy's-Own Saybrooke is entirely consistent with this British excellence. It has superb single-needle tailoring throughout, French cuffs, permanent collar days. 10.29*

**Splendid!**
Ties of silks and wools. In the 14th Century, when Chaucer penned his rolling verse, Ancient Silk Madders were dyed in much the same way the British follow today. Macy's has magnificent Madder ties for you in these noble colors and famous textures. And of course we have the patterned silk foulards and wool challis prints and solids. In short, we have the entire handsome company of ties that are as British as Bond Street. The Madders, 3.29. The silks and wools, 2.34

**Dapper!**
The cordovan shoe. A town shoe, as the British see it and build it, magnificently Here the Cambridge, a classic English cordovan wing tip in superlative leathers. 17.98

**Hello!**
Leather kits. Leather and London go together as naturally as Big Ben and Parliament. Shoe shine kit has 2 brushes, polish, cloths. 3.69. Military brush set, has brushes of pure bristle, 5.64. Utility kit has room for everything. 6.53

**Hear, Hear!**
The weskits. Two favorites born and bred in the colorful world of horses and racing, the sport of kings and Mr. Tattersall. His name still stands in London town and identifies our checked wool vest here. The solid woolen vest recalls the English coach boys and their hearty penchant for bright-buttoned weskits. British wools. Solid, 18.74. Tattersall, 10.94

**Brawny!**
*The knit pullover. When the British turn their hand to knit pullovers, you really get something special. Here's a woolen, shawl-collared pullover, a classic format with contemporary additions: the bulky wool and two buttons for snugness against chill. Thank the British for thinking of you. 29.91*

**Boot Mon!**
The tartan robe. As welcome to a man as a crackling fire on a cold day. The authentic tartan patterns of our casual robe are inspired by the highlands, loomed in rich English wools for comfort and warmth, with shawl collar and handy patch pockets. Americans adopt it on sight. 19.98

**Jolly good!**
The muffler. A highland fling in the best tradition: our British muffler of true tartans in bold, glowing colors. The fabric, a British blend of 70% cashmere, 30% wool. The soft texture, unique. 7.04

**Tip-top!**
Two hats, one cap. The hats are made expressly and exclusively for us by Joshua Turner, famous London hatter. The classic black bowler is here to stay, it's as British as the Bank of England. The medium grey homburg now has a higher, neater crown and a narrow brim. The natty cap is a plucky tweed, that lively, springy hand-woven wool that stands up to the damp, a British institution in itself. The hats, each 12.69. The cap, 5.99

**Corking!**
*The Barracuta raincoat. Only a foggy day is more British than raincoats made in England. Barracuta has tailored this one splendidly, with raglan sleeves, slash pockets. And the knowledgeable British include a zip-in all-wool liner for the windy, sleety days they meet so bravely. The coat is cotton gabardine. '55*

**Smashing!**
Viyella sport shirts. Britain's historic Scottish clans provide the tartan patterns; Britain's famous looms produce the fabrics. The fine blend is 55% lambswool, 45% cotton; famous for lightweight and warmth. They're washable, and the authentic tartan patterns have British integrity, won't fade. 19.95

You'll hail Macy's magnificent new Men's Store too where you will find the best of everything British, the samplings on this page and ever so much more. Everything in the best Macy tradition of great, generous assortments, and a strict standing policy of thrift. No wonder Macy's sells more British goods than any other store outside the Commonwealth.

*The simple severity of the illustrations and copy contrasted to the very busy masthead gives this page its visual drama. This ad, like the others, could have been a lead ad of an entire campaign, yet collectively all the ads held together.*

157

## WHY IS THIS AD APPEARING TODAY IN BOTH STOCKHOLM AND NEW YORK?

## VARFÖR PUBLICERAS DENNA ANNONS I DAG BÅDE I NEW YORK OCH STOCKHOLM?

Två stora varuhus i två stora städer berättar i dag om varandra för sina kunder. Vi är nämligen båda på det klara med att shopping är hälften av nöjet att resa utrikes. Antingen man ägnar sig åt att samla rena minnessaker eller åt att köpa sådant man inte finner där hemma, är den största tjusningen med att shoppa i främmande land att iaktta hur och vad andra kvinnor köper. Det är ett underbart sätt att lära sig hur ett folk lever, vad man där drömmer om och önskar sig...och en massa som man aldrig hittar i resehandböckerna. Välj därför när Ni är utomlands det varuhus som är särskilt typiskt, som har allt Ni vill se...likaom dessa båda, två varuhus som länge haft nära och vänskapliga förbindelser med varandra. Här ber vi att var för sig få presentera kollegan för våra egna kunder.

**Shoppa hos Nordiska — och köam "Stockholms puls"**...Så ungefär uttrycker sig en Amerikan med kända och spridda resehandböcker hos Europa ...och säger också: "Det fabulösa NK (Förkortning för Nordiska Kompaniet) är en lika fornämig turistattraktion som Slottet och Stadshuset—en institution så fascinerande att ingen turist som någonsin hört talas om den bunde dedeens om att förtiga den...ett måste för den som ger sig ut på shopping." Ja, NK är ett måste för Er. Det är inte bara Sveriges största och förnämsta varuhus...det är det rätta stället för att bekanta sig med svenskarnas livsföring på den som konkurrens högt smakmod som beundras världen över... NK är ett julbrudstäl varuhus. Och det är lika väbent för att inns urval av glas och keramik som för sina moderna hemmiböbinge...for sin delikata mat som för allt överrättliga ledarskap på dam- och herrmodets område.

P.S. Välkomna. Fru finkom och hom New Yorker och köéna på oss i NK för att se reda på oss hur som är ortendinst... eller si. Väl i Stockholm bona? Ni ipis NK. Den turneula pärreklosken med NK:s märke högt över oss, pak år synlig i hela staden och en halfvje.

**Shop Nordiska — "the heartbeat of Stockholm"**...This is a quotation from one of the most well-informed and widely circulated American guide-books on Europe...which further states that "Fabulous NK (short for Nordiska Kompaniet) is just as solid a sightseeing attraction as the Royal Palace and the Town Hall—an institution so fascinating that no visitor who knows about it ever dreams of missing it...a must for any shop-hound." Yes, NK is a must for you. It is not only the biggest, finest and most important store in Sweden ...it is the place to get acquainted with the Swedish way of living on that unrivalled high taste level which is admired the world over...NK is a complete story. And it is just as well-known for its splendid selection of glass and ceramics as for its contemporary home furnishings...for its delicious foods as well as for its supreme leadership in ladies' and men's fashions.

P.S. Now, Mrs. Miss and Mr. New Yorker, please come and see us in NK, and find out whether we have overstated...or not. Once in Stockholm you can't miss NK. The great revolving clock high above us on the top is a "beacon" visible all over the city.

**In New York, shop where New Yorkers shop...Macy's**. You could spend your whole vacation here...and still not see everything. That's how big the world's biggest store is. But Macy's is more than a store. It's part of what makes New York the unique city it is, a landmark...like the Empire State Building or the Brooklyn Bridge. There's always something going on at Macy's, so no matter when you come you'll enjoy just strolling the aisles and looking. And, when you get down to serious shopping, you'll discover that "It's Smart to Be Thrifty" makes sense in any tongue. Most of Macy's goods, from prosaic cookers to petticoats, are cost where you can see them. Or, if you'd rather, Macy's Personal Shoppers (who talk your language—and we speak some 40 others as well) will be glad to guide you. So be a New Yorker for a day... spend it, as so many New Yorkers do, at Macy's.

P.S. For New Yorkers going abroad: Macy's has tons of just about everything for your trip, from the right clothes, to good advice.

**I New York — shoppa där New York shoppar...Macy's**...Ni skulle kunna tillbringa hela Er semester där...utan att ändå ha sett allting. Det säger hur stort världens största varuhus är. Men Macy's är mer än ett varuhus. Det är en del av det som gör New York till den enastående stad det är, en blickpunkt ...som Empire State Building eller Brooklyn Bridge. Det händer alltid något hos Macy's och det spelar därför ingen roll när Ni kommer in. Det är alltid lika roligt att ströva omkring och bara titta. Och när det verkligen blir fråga om att köpa kommer Ni att upptäcka att Macy's slogan "It's smart to be thrifty" (närmast: "Det är klokt att vara ekonomisk") har en innebörd på varje språk. De alla flesta av Macy's varor, från trivsthäxkar till underkläder, finns framme för Ett skärskådande. Om Ni så hellre vill, blir Ni personligen omhändertagen av Macy's huvudpünst (vart slab av "shoppers" talar ensenka-och 40 andra språk därtill). Bli New Yorkare för en dag...tillbringa den som så många New York-bor gör—hos Macy's.

P.S. För New York-bor som far utomlands har Macy's massor av praktisk allt för Er resa, från de rätta kläderna till goda råd.

NEW YORK TIMES (AUX GALERIES LAFAYETTE)

## POURQUOI CETTE ANNONCE PARAIT-ELLE AUJOURD'HUI SIMULTANEMENT A NEW YORK ET A PARIS?

## WHY IS THIS AD APPEARING TODAY IN BOTH PARIS AND NEW YORK?

Two great stores in two great cities are telling their customers about each other today because we both realize that shopping is half the fun of going abroad, no matter which way you cross the Atlantic. Whether you spend your time collecting souvenirs or things you can't get at home, the greatest enchantment of shopping in a foreign land is watching how and what other women buy. It's a wonderful way to learn how a country lives, its dreams and its hopes...and a lot of things that never get into the guide books. So be sure, when you're abroad, that you shop in the store that's uniquely typical, the store that has everything you want...like these two stores, two stores who have long had a close and friendly relationship. Now each of us would like to introduce our customers to the other.

*When a campaign has a point of difference that has to be dramatized, all other elements in the campaign should be as constant as possible, so that the point of difference will be as quickly apparent to the reader as possible.*

*These four ads were part of a series which was called the "YOU" campaign. The objective of the campaign was to emphasize the importance of the individual customer in a store that serves over 150,000 a day. This philosophy was expressed in every ad, with minor variations, as follows: "That's Macy's. A store so big we have something (although clearly, not the same thing) for everyone. A store with a philosophy. It may not be important as the law of gravity... but we believe in it: Macy's has only one customer... YOU. Maybe that's why we have more customers than anybody else". The campaign characteristic over and above the consistent copy approach was the unusual type treatment with dotted arrows leading from copy block to copy block plus a decorative cartoon illustration drawn on a flat plane. The campaign, however, had this additional excitement, each ad had extra consumer interest because every situation was as contemporary as that day's newspaper.*

# You hitched their wagon to the stars

The next hundred years...and the stars...belong to your children. They may all grow up to see the Moon explored, maybe Mars colonized. Yes, the future belongs to them. But they won't all do the same thing in the future...and they can't all be alike. For while you can chart the orbit of a satellite...you can't chart the orbit of a child.

One boy will be professor of astronautics in a college still unfounded. The little one next to him will write a folk opera set on the Moon. And the girl in the pony tail? Her sequinned space suits will revolutionize fashion.

**How does Macy's know?**

In our first hundred years, we've seen a lot of changes...seen frontiers shift from the untamed West to the unexplored skies, seen science fiction become science. But we realize there's one thing that never changes: the individuality of people.

And children are individuals.

You hear a lot of talk about patterns of behavior. Or look around and see what seems like a uniform on every kid in sight. Or watch them switch from one hero to another...en masse. But you know that your child is different from all other children. And so do we. To Macy's, 60 youngsters, each riding a bike in chinos, loafers and white socks are 60 different people.

That's why it's so satisfying to shop at Macy's. We recognize your child's right to be interested in physics or sculpture...and always have. We suspect that some of today's scientists got their first chemistry sets or their first steam engines in Macy's Hobby Shop...a fascinating (and complete) world of plane models, butterfly mountings, paints, photo equipment, chemical outfits, etching sets, geological specimens and just about every other branch of the physical sciences and the arts. Because nothing in this shop is a toy. Some of it is simplified ...but it all works.

Or take Macy's Camp Shop. We know how many blankets are needed in Maine and what's worn at co-ed dances in the Berkshires. We know because we've been fitting out campers with everything from sweaters to canteens for generations. Official outfitters for 185 camps, Macy's assortment of camp gear is astronomic...but not our prices.

That's Macy's. A store so big we have something (although, clearly, not the same thing) for everyone. A store with a philosophy. It may not be as important as the law of gravity...but we believe in it: Macy's has only one customer...you. Maybe that's why we have more customers than anybody else.

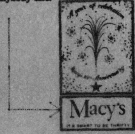

**Macy's**
IT'S SMART TO BE THRIFTY

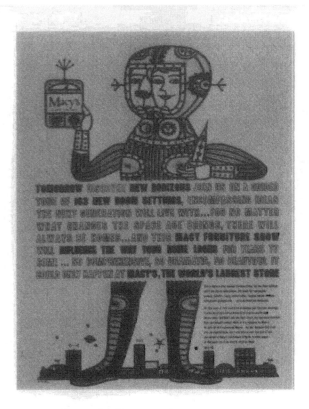

Every element in this ad reflects the campaign characteristics of the ad on the opposite page. The copy changes and so does the illustration but the basic format does not.

Whenever possible, it is advisable to use one artist for a campaign. The artist's technique and interpretation helps maintain continuity. Walter Einsel, an artist of exceptional talent, designed this campaign.

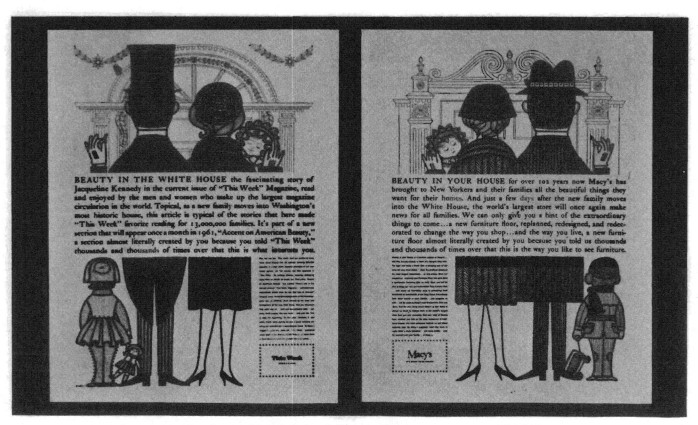

An opportunity that couldn't be missed. Practically the same day the Chief Executive and his family moved into the White House, a new furniture floor opens with news for every other family. An additional double truck was added to the schedule and treated with the same graphic technique to help maintain continuity for the campaign.

**TOMORROW** YOU AND 16,000,000 OTHER NEW YORKERS AND SUBURBAN NEW YORKERS ARE INVITED TO SEE **170 NEW ROOM SETTINGS** THAT WILL ONCE AGAIN CHANGE THE WAY NEW YORK LIVES...TWICE AS MANY AND ALL TWICE AS BEAUTIFUL AS EVER BECAUSE THIS IS **MACY'S 100th ANNIVERSARY** YEAR...AND THIS IS THE MOST EXTENSIVE, MOST HISTORIC **FURNITURE SHOW** IN ALL OUR 100 YEARS.

See the most important Furniture Show since Peter Stuyvesant governed New York. A show so big you could spend a week here and still not see everything. A world of intriguing room settings at Herald Square and the Macy branch store near you. And this is not only a fascinating show but a spectacular sale ... Macy's 100th Anniversary Furniture Sale. For the kind of buys you'll see tomorrow in Macy's Furniture Show and Sale ... see the other Macy pages in this paper.

Extra: at Herald Square only. Come at 2 p.m. to Macy's Decorating department, 9th floor, and join the guided tour of our room settings, led by a trained decorator. You'll learn a lot ... **and you'll love it.**

*A campaign of recognizable vigor. All elements in these ads are unusual, in technique, scale, and subject matter. Every prerequisite for a campaign is demonstrated in these ads. The newspaper reader doesn't have to be reminded that this is "#1 of a series". The campaign speaks for itself . . . loudly.*

The bursting fireworks was the primary symbol created for Macy's 100th Anniversary campaign. As it was to be a year long celebration, additional recognizable forms had to be introduced from time to time for flexibility. In one of the first ads of the campaign (above) a decorative proscenium frame was designed to help punctuate and distinguish each segment of the campaign.

One period of the campaign slid easily into the other, the "frame" was always changed to conform to the period and message of the campaign. In this one it reflects the treatment used on most early 1900 bandstands.

In this ad of the campaign, the "frame" was inspired by the copy line "The world's greatest theatre." The frame differs from the one on the left but the idea is the same.

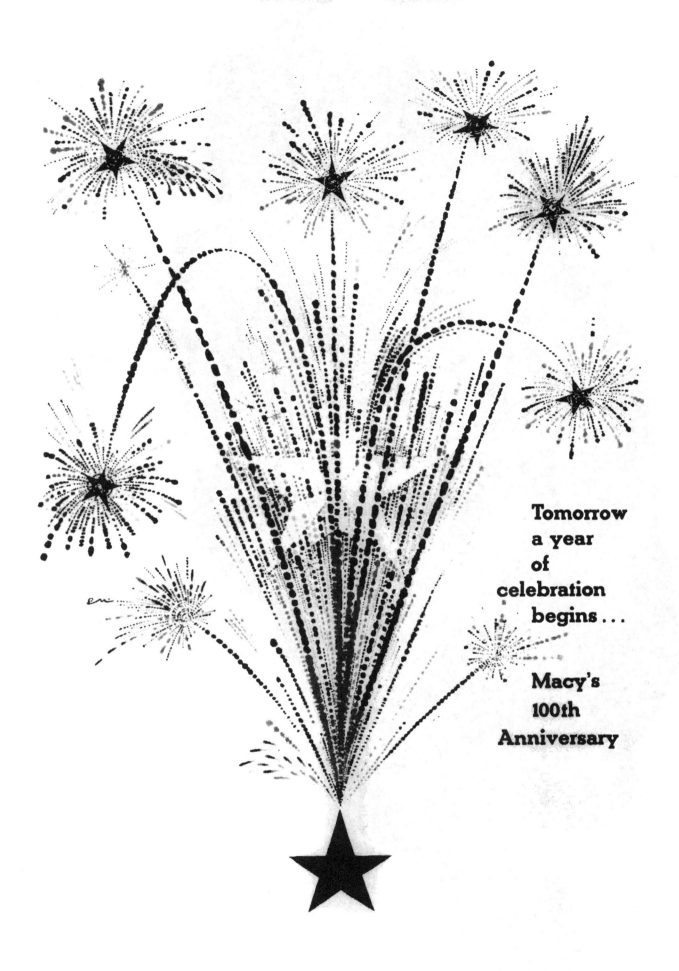

Tomorrow
a year
of
celebration
begins...

Macy's
100th
Anniversary

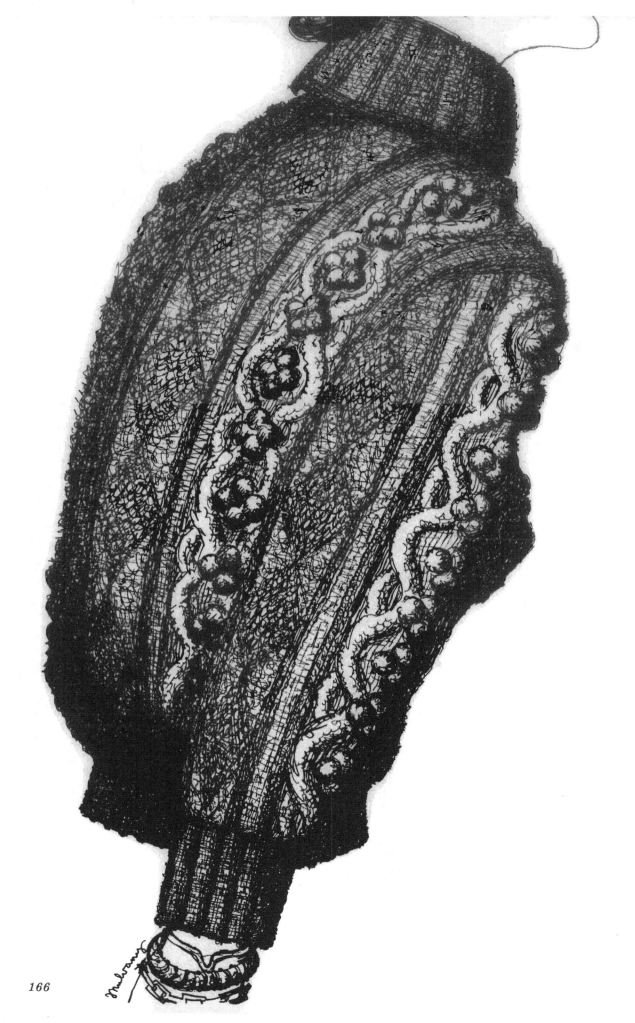

# ARTWORK

## *"It starts from the layout"*

### "It all started with the Egyptians"

A junior art director at Abraham & Straus many years ago made an interesting comment during a discussion on artwork techniques. He said: "There's nothing new. It all started with the Egyptians." The group shrugged off this profound, but naive, remark with a quick retort: "Yeah, but *they* didn't do newspaper advertising." The discussion then continued on the relative merits of one store's art technique versus another store's, and the meteoric rise of some artists with individual styles and their equally sudden demise. Nothing was really settled at this discussion It was typical of many informal gatherings of creative people when they meet to talk shop. But . . . was nothing really settled?

### Another profound observation

This happened in 1936. The Advertising Director of a large department store in Sydney, Australia, while on a tour of New York, dropped in to talk advertising with me. We talked of many things: merchandising differences, schedules, people, and particularly the appearance of advertising. As we were reviewing the latest ads, he made an offhand comment that startled me. "Do you realize," he remarked, "that the happiness and gaiety that were so apparent in your department store illustrations during the boom period of 1928 and 1929 were gone entirely in the doldrums of the depression? The smiles had disappeared, the expressions were all serious." As he spoke I realized that, consciously or subconsciously, we let the rise and fall of business influence the appearance of advertising and, particularly, the quality and technique of our illustrations.

### Two observations, two remarks

How does an art technique get started? Who originates it? Did it really begin "with the Egyptians?" Do business cycles affect art styles and techniques? These are all fascinating questions, all provoked by two casual remarks. I decided it would take too long to trace the history of artwork back to the Egyptians, but the history of artwork from 1928 on could be reviewed and some meaningful conclusions drawn. So I spent weeks going through eight years (1928-1935) of the Sunday issues of the New York Times.

I studied page after page of advertising, looking for common denominators. The conclusion became obvious. *The curve of business does, indeed, affect the curve and appearance of artwork.*

Good business and bad business conditions are the greatest factors, not only in the kind of artwork used, but also the amount of artwork in retail advertising. There are, of course, other significant and secondary factors that affect the art in the ads. The improvements in engraving and printing techniques, the changes in architectural styles, the creativity of new fashions, the popularity of new gallery painters and museum exhibits . . . these, too, have a profound effect and influence. But even these are directly related to the curve of business . . . good or bad.

In the next few pages you will see reproductions of ads taken from the files of the New York Times. The period covered is 1928-1935 . . . a complete cycle from the boom business of 1928-29, through one of the worst depressions in America's history, and then the beginning of recovery in 1934 and 1935.

*Note the art styles of 1928 and early 1929.*

*See the emphasis on price in the late 1929s and the de-emphasis on art.*

*Observe the start of photography and realism in artwork.*

*Mark the use of cartoons in retail advertising.*

*Notice the caricatured drawings of merchandise.*

*See an illustration of a man with a smile on his face and a golf club in his hand.*

*Watch for a new development in photography in retail advertising.*

*. . . and finally see a return to glamor in artwork.*

### What's happened since 1935?

Fortunately for all of us, there's been no return of "The Big Cycle."

Instead, there have been many "little cycles" of business change as well as changes in individual stores, industries, cities, states, areas, and the entire country In every case, the business change has been reflected by a sharper, more staccato change in the use of artwork and the kind of artwork seen in the pages of the newspaper.

In short, see a complete business cycle and how it affected the advertising artwork of that period.

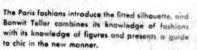

*September 1929*

Kurzman ad: The illustration is idealized, understated. There is no realism, no detail. Business was booming, people were buying . . . it was a seller's market. The illustrations reflected the attitude of the times.

*September 1929*

BEST & CO. AD: The elongated figures are at least 8 heads high, the drawings purely decorative. The haughty expressions seem to be saying "The stock market is going up to the sky." It did ... until October 1929.

*October 1931*

SAKS-34TH ST. AD: 1930 was a year of
confusion. No clear picture was apparent, no clear way out of the depression.
In 1931 prices became bigger, the artwork
more realistic. Obviously, customers were
buying on the basis of value.

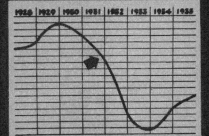

*December 1931*

LAMBERT BROS. AD: This is the beginning of the consistent use of photography in newspaper advertising. Its appeal to the customer was one of truth. "A photograph doesn't lie." It shows the product as it actually is. (Note, too, the price emphasis in the Finchley and Whitehouse & Hardy ads.)

**2.50**
a special price
**NEW
SWEATER**

LORD & TAYLOR
FIFTH AVENUE

Dyed Blue Fox
in both *quantity*
and *quality*, on this
new coat at . . .
**76.00**

LORD & TAYLOR
FIFTH AVENUE

## LORD & TAYLOR'S
young new yorkers' shop
has some Merry-Merry Prices

FOR THE
COMING
HOLIDAYS!

25.00

16.50

25.00

16.50

FIFTH FLOOR
LORD & TAYLOR

*Special*
**1.70**

*so give her two pairs of*
**Crepe or Leather
Slippers**

LORD & TAYLOR
FIFTH AVENUE

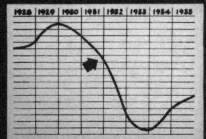

*December 1931*

LORD & TAYLOR ADS: A concerted effort
was made on the part of all merchants.
"Let's try to pull ourselves out of this
mess." This is reflected in the use of fun
illustrations, a transition between decorative drawings, realism and cartoons. (Note
the ad on the lower left).

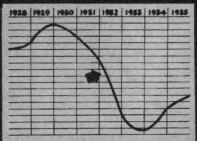

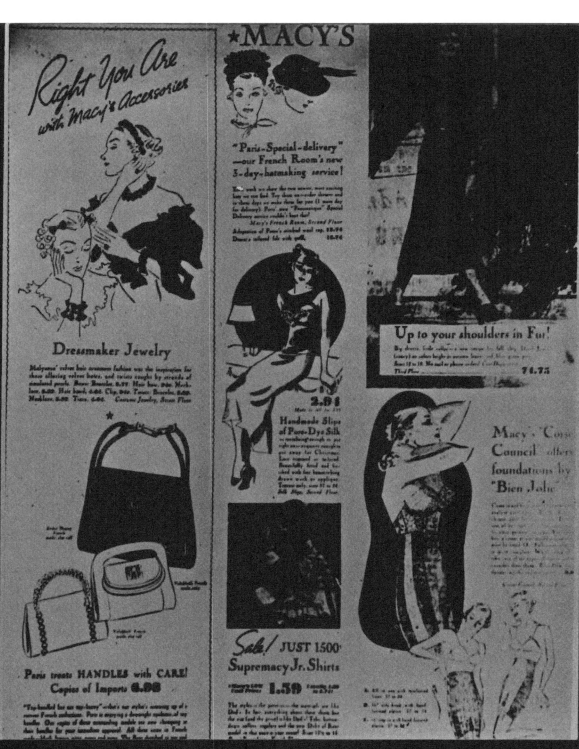

*October 1933*

MACY'S MEN'S STORE AD: The first illustration noted in a couple of years of men with smiles on their faces. They're holding golf clubs . . . and during the 1929-32 period, playing golf was an inexcusable extravagance. Note the realism in the art treatment, a tendency that continues.

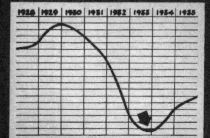

# TODAY'S DECOR

**THIS IS THE DELPHINIUM ROOM**

— one of the series of interesting and colorfully decorated rooms just opened on our Seventh Floor. It's done in tones, from soft delphinium mauves through lavendered blue to a deep strong blue. In it we have put this white modernized Directoire dining room with the deep blue note in the upholstery of the chairs. Spots of crystal lift the whole effect to an unusual brilliance. The nine piece dining room group 695.00

*Lord & Taylor*
SEVENTH FLOOR

## IT'S IMPORTANT TO KNOW IT'S A *Lord & Taylor* COAT

*January 1934*

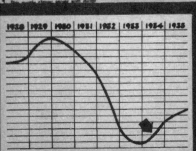

LORD & TAYLOR ADS: The business trend starts on its way up. Value is still important, but people are beginning to live again and there's great interest in "fixing up the home," women are becoming interested in fashion rather than just in prices. Note the illustrations rather than the single figure with no atmosphere.

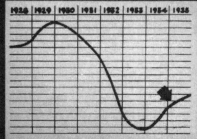

*December 1934*

LORD & TAYLOR AD: Business is going well and customers are buying. The mood is "Let's get dressed up and go places." The artwork reflects the photographic realism of the times, but as interpreted by artists, with a decorative interplay for graphic interest.

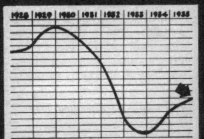

*December 1935*

BONWIT TELLER AD: Business in department
stores in 1935 was reported as being 2 to 60%
ahead of the previous year's. The business cycle
and the art cycle have come almost the full
round. Note the return to the vague elongated
drawing with its lack of detail in the cape in
this ad. Customers no longer have to be shown
every stitch and button because money is easier.

## Advertising experts

When Louis Tannenbaum was Advertising Manager of Macy's New York, he had a drawer full of buttons imprinted "Advertising Expert!" in bright red ink.

These buttons were presented to merchandise executives at appropriate occasions, usually during a heated debate over a difference of opinion about an ad. The presentation of the button was made in jest, to break the tension . . . but it had serious overtones. For Mr. Tannenbaum knew from long experience that everyone considers himself an advertising expert, especially an expert of art work.

Some merchandise executives do have the ability to judge a piece of art and recommend improvements, many don't.

Their interests are almost always personal. It's their merchandise, or their ad, or their favorite manufacturer's ad, or it's their competition that has to be emulated or beaten. Hence it's *their ad.* Yet personal likes and dislikes, while important, should not be the prime consideration in creating a store's advertising appearance.

The art style, like the advertising format for a store, should be created to reflect the character, the merchandise, and the policies of the store. Within this context, of course, personal opinions are warranted and even desirable for better understanding and improvement.

## Creating an art style

The art techniques used to create a store's art style must be tailored to fit the needs of the store. Before creating the art style four major factors should be considered and many questions answered.

1. *The art market in your city.*

   Are artists available? Are good artists available? Are they flexible so that they can give you an individualized style? Are art students available for training?

2. *The competition in your city.*

   What art style does your major competitor use? How different should your art style be? Should it be better? In what way?

3. *The quality of reproduction in your papers.*

   Is the printing poor? Good? Excellent? Do soft edge wash drawings print with a hard outline? Do photographs print muddy? Must special art techniques be devised to insure good reproduction?

4. *The art work budget.*

   How much can you afford to spend? Is your budget too low? Adequate? What guide do you use for the proper amount of artwork dollars?

Answer these questions and you will have a realistic basis with which to start creating an art style for your store.

It's highly desirable for a store to have an individual and recognizable art style A large store or, more specifically, a large advertiser can use more than one art technique for flexibility, but the smaller store should forego this advantage for the greater reward of consumer recognition of its advertising.

## Art for art's sake

Don't use art for the sake of having a picture in an ad. Some ads require art, some don't. Artwork costs money, takes time to prepare, and uses newspaper space.

It's a natural tendency for most designers to start an ad with the art. It's natural because most advertising designers were trained as artists, not as ad makers.

It's equally natural for most merchants to request art in their ads. They, too, want to show their merchandise, and they, too, are not trained ad makers.

■ *Art should be used only when necessary: for merchandise information, to create emotion or drama, or as an innovation.*

The word "Paris" in an ad will say more, and conjure up a more exciting picture in the mind of a customer, than a drawing of the Eiffel Tower.

"Oriental Rugs" as part of a headline on an ad of rug listings gives a broader mental picture of the East than the conventional spot drawing of a camel in an oriental market place.

A stack of sheets, as shown in many ads, doesn't help the customer visualize the silky smoothness of 200 count percale. So why a drawing?

■ *If the artwork doesn't fill a specific and useful objective, don't use art.*

Artwork, however, is important. Take just sheets, for example: many stacks of sheets in an ad will give an impression of a great assortment.

A closeup drawing of a flower print sheet gives the ad reader information that would take many words to describe, and the words would not be as satisfactory as the drawing.

A drawing of a well-arranged and completely filled linen closet will suggest to a woman that she ought to fill her own linen closet.

Fitted sheets are a point of difference and require an illustration for customer information.

A white sheet on an elegant bed in a luxurious room setting can create an emotion; emotion can help sell more goods.

A cartoon or a decorative drawing of very tall people will create a mental picture of extra-large sheets faster than the numbers 108 x 122½.

These are just a few examples. The principles can be extended to include every ad and every classification of merchandise:

■ *Don't use art for the sake of having a picture in the ad—use art only when necessary to fill a specific need.*

## What is good artwork?

It was previously noted that, within the context of a store's established art style, there can be personal opinions on individual pieces of art. In fact, this is desirable for better understanding and improvement.

But when the question is raised, "Is it a good drawing?", as many personal opinions are offered as there are persons. It's probably natural that it should be so. For art in any form is personal, whether it's a painting, a ceramic, or even so-called commercial art used by department stores.

## An era of sophistication

The public—you and I—is more sophisticated today than ever before. All forms of communication . . . newspapers, television, magazines, movies, museums, theatre . . . have helped raise this level of sophistication. What was understandable and good communication 20 years ago might be considered "corny" or "square" today. How does this relate to art in department store advertising?

Showing every stitch, seam, and button in a drawing of a dress is not necessarily the best selling technique today, yet showing every detail in a stereo circuit is.

Showing and emphasizing a minuscule change in a beltline or skirtline in a drawing could be the difference between a drawing and a fashion drawing which is much more desirable.

A good fashion drawing should give fashion information and make the reader want to look and feel like the woman in the illustration. She's not wearing a stereo circuit but a wonderful new fashion. The best proof that this type of drawing is effective is dramatically demonstrated by the change in the mail order catalogue business. Here the customer has to buy from illustrations only, because she can't come in to try on the dress. Yet look, for example, at the last five Spiegel & Co.'s catalogues, a far cry from the old catalogue type of illustration. Instead, significant points of fashion are stressed and illustrated in the manner of the best fashion magazines . . . and Spiegel's fashion business has flourished.

Sometimes a fashion illustration is not enough. Recently a fashion merchandise man and a sales promotion executive were wondering why a new and beautifully shaped handbag didn't sell as well as expected after a large ad in the newspaper. The bags were well illustrated. The copy was descriptive of the new long shape of the bag. They finally came to an interesting conclusion because (a) The scale of the bag wasn't shown. The customer couldn't tell whether it was a little clutch or a giant bag. (b) The customer wasn't shown how the bag should be carried. This bag was planned to be tucked under the arm, not carried in the hand. The ad didn't show it.

We all find ourselves in the same trap. "Show the merchandise and it should sell". Perhaps it ought to be "Show the merchandise in use (if the use is new) and it *will* sell". Especially a new item with a new way of using it.

Furniture merchandise men know that sofas, chairs, bedrooms, dining rooms, etc. sell 3 to 5 times better when shown in a room setting in their stores. Women can see the scale better, can visualize it as it might look in their own homes. Yet most furniture ads show individual items with very little or no room atmosphere. "Don't confuse the merchandise with atmosphere" they say. And they help defeat their own purpose. No individual or thing exists in a vacuum. Every piece of furniture, accessory, wearing apparel—everything a customer buys, wears or uses—has a definite relationship to the way the customer lives. *The proper amount of atmosphere in the art will enhance the merchandise.*

## Good art doesn't always have to be realistic

Merchandise or an idea, or both, can be sold effectively with non-realistic art. Of course, we tend to think of decorative or impressionistic artwork primarily in connection with non-merchandise or institutional advertising. It's probably correct to think of it in these terms, for this is the area where stores deliberately decide to be different or provocative. Yet the very store that runs such a series wouldn't dare try merchandise ads with an abstract art treatment. And they may be right in not doing so. However, many stores are using a decorative art technique and using it successfully to show and sell goods.

Practically every drawing used in newspaper advertising today is in some sense a decorative drawing. Even photographs, the realistic medium, are no longer absolutely realistic. As previously observed, the realistic drawing technique of the mail order catalogue of 25 years ago is gone. It has outlived its usefulness. People are too sophisticated for it today.

What is the decorative drawing you find in today's advertising? A flat plane of wash on a fashion figure with a few outline brush strokes is decorative. A posterized tonal quality over a piece of furniture makes it a decorative drawing. A group of shoes, gloves, and jewelry on a plane that couldn't exist in nature is a decorative drawing. Readers don't question it. They like it and buy from it. It's thoughtful, interesting and contemporary.

## What, then, is good artwork?

■ *Good artwork is artwork that suits the store, that fills a necessary function in the ad, that communicates to the customer clearly and quickly. Good artwork is contemporary, significant in what it tells the customer. Good artwork creates a desire to buy. In short, it does an effective selling job.*

MAX WALTER, the dean of interior fashion artists, draws furniture and surrounds it with a room setting of great charm.

ALVIN PIMSLER draws men's fashions with flair and sophistication. The total impression is more important than the details.

MEYER KLING "paints" a still life with his camera. The grey values are kept simple for best newspaper reproduction.

CARL WILSON, a great illustrator, does fashion drawings of charming people in interesting situations to create a mood.

From Bettman Archives collection of old engravings . . . decorative spots that can enhance an ad if used judiciously.

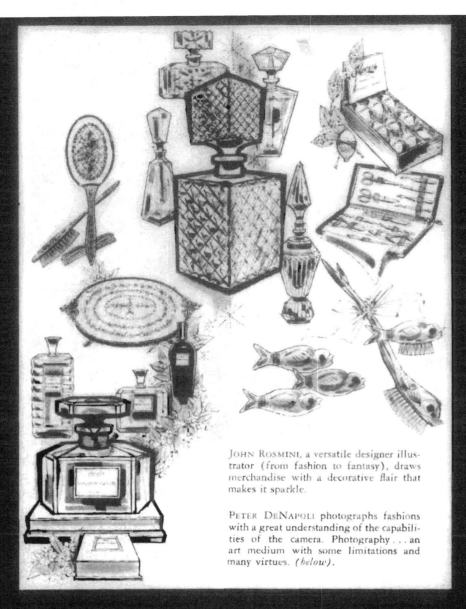

DOROTHY CHINITZ, a specialist in children's illustrations, draws them with charm, poise, dignity and "fashion."

JOHN ROSMINI, a versatile designer illustrator (from fashion to fantasy), draws merchandise with a decorative flair that makes it sparkle.

PETER DeNAPOLI photographs fashions with a great understanding of the capabilities of the camera. Photography . . . an art medium with some limitations and many virtues. *(below)*.

KENNETH RICHARDS, a designer artist with a rare sense of humor, illustrates here that 108 x 122½ is indeed an extra long sheet (see page 180).

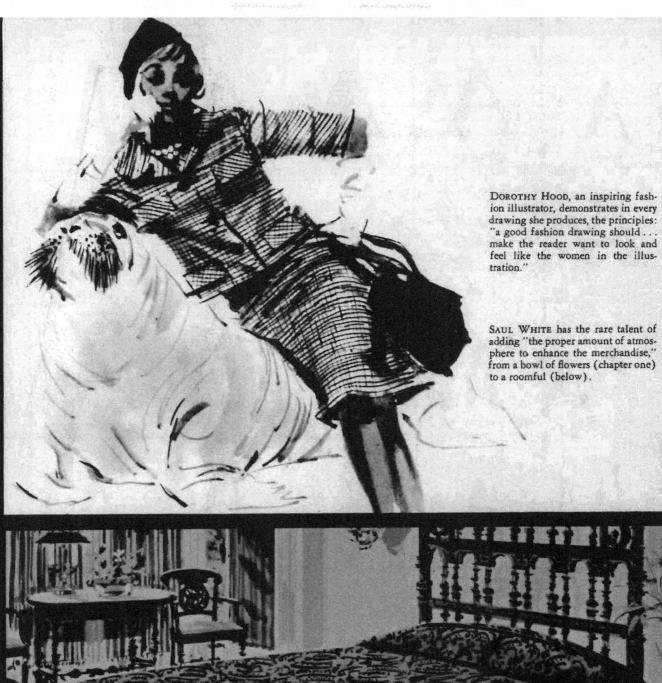

DOROTHY HOOD, an inspiring fashion illustrator, demonstrates in every drawing she produces, the principles: "a good fashion drawing should . . . make the reader want to look and feel like the women in the illustration."

SAUL WHITE has the rare talent of adding "the proper amount of atmosphere to enhance the merchandise," from a bowl of flowers (chapter one) to a roomful (below).

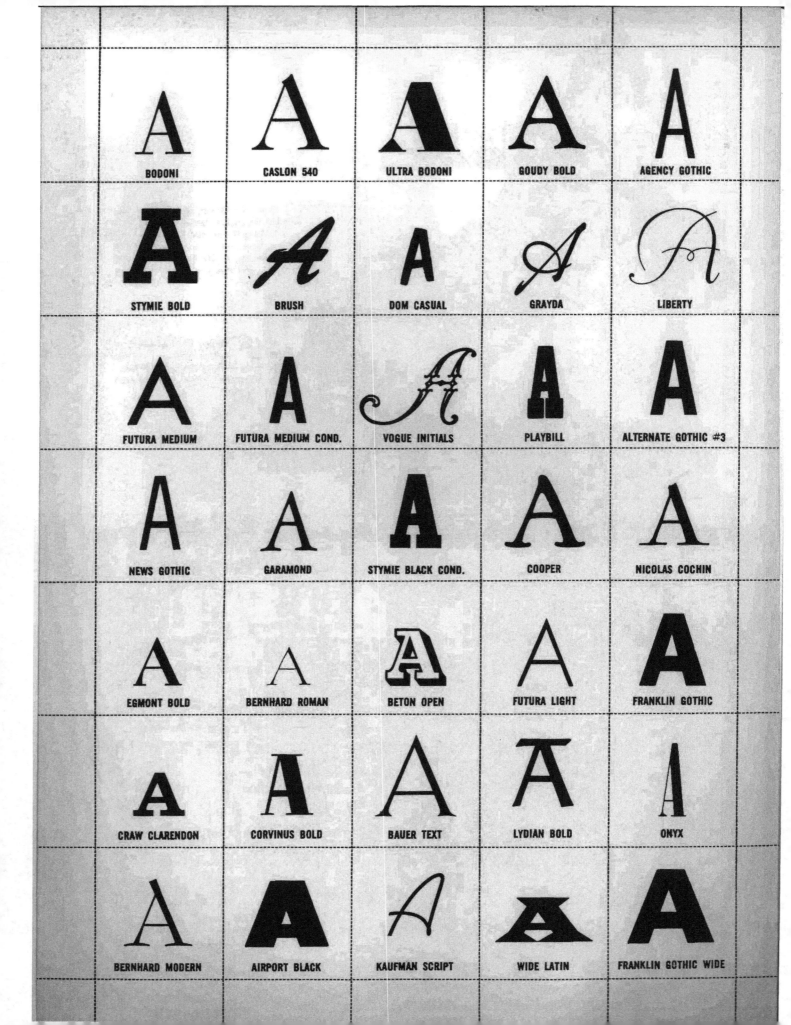

| | | | | |
|---|---|---|---|---|
| **A**<br>BODONI | **A**<br>CASLON 540 | **A**<br>ULTRA BODONI | **A**<br>GOUDY BOLD | **A**<br>AGENCY GOTHIC |
| **A**<br>STYMIE BOLD | *A*<br>BRUSH | **A**<br>DOM CASUAL | *A*<br>GRAYDA | *A*<br>LIBERTY |
| **A**<br>FUTURA MEDIUM | **A**<br>FUTURA MEDIUM COND. | *A*<br>VOGUE INITIALS | **A**<br>PLAYBILL | **A**<br>ALTERNATE GOTHIC #3 |
| **A**<br>NEWS GOTHIC | **A**<br>GARAMOND | **A**<br>STYMIE BLACK COND. | **A**<br>COOPER | **A**<br>NICOLAS COCHIN |
| **A**<br>EGMONT BOLD | **A**<br>BERNHARD ROMAN | **A**<br>BETON OPEN | **A**<br>FUTURA LIGHT | **A**<br>FRANKLIN GOTHIC |
| **A**<br>CRAW CLARENDON | **A**<br>CORVINUS BOLD | **A**<br>BAUER TEXT | **A**<br>LYDIAN BOLD | **A**<br>ONYX |
| **A**<br>BERNHARD MODERN | **A**<br>AIRPORT BLACK | *A*<br>KAUFMAN SCRIPT | **A**<br>WIDE LATIN | **A**<br>FRANKLIN GOTHIC WIDE |

# TYPOGRAPHY

## "*It starts to make sense*"

### TYPE IS TO READ

Researchers tell us they estimate the average person in North America is exposed to 1,200 commercial print messages a day...

More and more people are wearing corrective eye glasses than ever before (especially the over-40-year-old market). What's your guess as to the percentage of people using glasses today? 20%, 30%, 40%? Think again. It's 54% of everybody over 6 years old in the United States—more than 85 million people.

A company is marketing a watch with enlarged numerals for easier reading...

Insurance companies are eliminating the "fine print" in policy contracts...

New York State passed a law in which it specifies that installment contracts must be set in type no smaller than 8 point and certain phrases must be set no smaller than 8 point boldface...

Even the numbers on the telephone dials have gotten bigger.

Which leads us to the inevitable and obvious conclusion that the primary function of typography is to get itself read. Every other consideration must, therefore, be secondary.

### TYPE IS A GRAPHIC ELEMENT

Most artists who become "layout artists" aren't trained to recognize the relationship of type to picture in an ad, nor do they always recognize that type itself is an interesting graphic element. Unfortunately, the tendency is to indicate the position of the art in the ad, then try to find an area in which to fit the type. This technique is just as unsound as the opposite—that of indicating the type areas first and then filling in with the art. The best way, therefore, is to consider art and type as equally important graphic elements which should receive equal consideration when designing the ad.

### *Equal consideration does not mean equal space.*

Just as the artist's tendency is to dramatize the art, the writer's tendency is to tell the story as completely as possible. Thus, the inevitable conflict. Should the art be made smaller, so that more copy (type) can be used—or should the copy be cut—or set in smaller type?

This problem can be resolved in a number of ways.

1. Make the decision of copy or art emphasis for each ad as the problem arises. This leaves your staff wide open to a conflict on every ad.
2. Solve the problem when creating your store advertising style—and specify that the objective is 75% art to 25% copy, or any proportion that suits your individual philosophy. This gives your staff a simple rule for most of your ads, with individual problem ads to be resolved as they arise.

Even with a clear cut overall philosophy, the conflict will arise—as the objective of individual ads change. For instance—a Spring flower hat ad may require 5 or 6 lines of copy and 3 or 4 different styles of hats. Obviously, art emphasis in this ad will do the best selling job. Yet a clearance of millinery in which all kinds of hats are being offered for sale, would require type emphasis and very little or no art. These are the two extremes; the conflict arises when the objective of the ad is not as apparent. The decision as to art or type emphasis must then be made jointly by the ad designer and the writer—in their best judgment and from the facts—which treatment will be the greatest service to the reader.

3. If the art is most important give *it* the space necessary—if the story (the type) is most important give *it* the space. "Remember, if you try to feature all you will feature none" (Chapter 6). The weakest decision graphically is a 50-50 compromise.

### TYPE IS ELOCUTION IN PRINT

A good typographic designer is like a good radio announcer. The unseen announcer has only his voice to express himself. He can shout for emphasis, whisper for effect—wheedle, preach, bluster, chatter.

The ad designer can do the same with type. He can use bold type for emphasis, light face to whisper—he can use a classic type face for one effect—he can use modern faces for another—he can intermix type faces for effect. His opportunity for variation is as great as his creativity and his knowledge of type faces.

The pity is that most ad makers don't read the copy for thought before they design it in an ad. They lay out the words and not the message. Here's a simple heading set 5 different ways all in the same type family (Caslon)—note the difference created by a slight typographic change of pace.

# THIS IS FOR YOU, MOTHER
## This is for *you*, Mother
### THIS *is for you, Mother*
#### *This is for* YOU, *mother*
##### *This is for you,* MOTHER

## FASHION IN TYPE AND TYPE FORMATS

There are thousands of type faces and families of type. The illustration on page 186 shows you a few. The possibilities of type combinations are infinite. Light face, bold face, Outline, Inline, Classic, Modern, Serif, Sans Serif, Condensed faces, Expanded faces, and many others. Some have subtle differences, some are radically different. (Note the type used in this chapter and how it differs from the other type styles used in the other chapters of the book.)

The type family used in an ad is important—but even more important is how the type is used, whatever the type chosen. For years we have heard and read that certain type faces should be used for elegant and fashionable ads, and that certain other type faces should be used for heavy machinery; because certain types convey a feeling of lightness, elegance, etc., and others are heavy and hard. Maybe they sometimes do convey this feeling, but in the judgment of experienced type and advertising designers, nothing is further from the truth. Any type face or family of types can be used successfully for any advertising message. It depends solely on the way the type is used in the ad. One could then argue— why all the type faces? And the question would be a valid one.

The answer, however, is that while a good designer can make any type work in any ad—some types can convey the graphic idea desired more easily or faster than others. Certain type faces, however, suddenly become the "fashionable" type to use (even creative advertising designers become conformists.)

For years the classic type faces like Caslon, Bodoni, and Garamond were the favorites—then came the unorthodox "Broadway" with a whole raft of strange faces that filled the pages of newspapers and magazines. The fashion changed when the modern Futuras, Stymies and Gothics followed—all clean, uncluttered, readable type—and now the fashion is swinging back to the Condensed Cheltenham, Clarendon, Century, Bodoni and Caslon.

The type fashion starts in a simple way...a designer who realizes that his ads are beginning to look like everyone else's needs a point of difference. So he decides to take a good long look at all the type faces that are available to him—or gets a brochure of a new type that's available, and uses it. If the ad or campaign is graphically outstanding— hundreds of other designers make a mental note of it and use the same type as quickly as they can. Suddenly a long neglected or brand new type face becomes fashionable. Not only does the type face become fashionable, but the graphic arrangement of the type becomes a cliché too...

For years, the traditional square block of copy was the only way to set type (as a matter of record, Percy Varian, a master typographer and production man, says that..."years ago the stores would send in great masses of straight matter to be set in 8 or 10 pt. type, all in one, two, possibly three measures only...proofs would be submitted in galley form...and a layout made up to accommodate the copy..."). Then came the freer line-for-line setting with each line of type offset to the right or left of the line above. Today the "fashion" is the unexpected measure of type—extraordinarily wide, or unusually narrow.

These "new fashions" of type and type use are a good and healthy sign. It shows that more interest is being shown in type as a graphic element. It shows that good advertising design is an integration—of the art and the type, each supplementing and supporting the other.

## THE ALL TYPE AD

It's a long time since the Greek historian, Herodotus, said, "A picture is worth a thousand words," but our guess is that if he worked in the advertising department of a retail store today he would realize how unsound that statement is.

If this refutation of an accepted premise still needs proof, consider just these two examples:

1. What kind of a drawing or photograph will say very quickly "50% wool, 25% acrilan, and the remaining 25% various fibers"?
2. What illustration will say quickly in a black and white newspaper ad "this dress comes in 12 colors including pink, blue and aqua"?

Marshall Field and Company ran a full page ad when the White Sox won the pennant in 1959 with just three words of copy, "You did it".

Macy's opened its 100th Anniversary with a full page illustration and just 9 words of copy—"Tomorrow a year of celebration begins...Macy's 100th Anniversary" (see page 165).

Many stores, from time to time have run ads with 1, 2, 5 or 10 words of copy, but it's a very rare ad that will run with absolutely no copy.

Ads without art—all type ads—however, are being printed practically every day in the newspapers throughout the country. An all type ad has a special quality about it. A quality of statesmanship, editorial, urgency.

Stores use "all type" ads for many reasons and many occasions:

1. A change in store policy.
2. A store event with a listing of many items.
3. An urgent message that must get in the paper quickly.
4. An institutional campaign of any size.
5. A clearance ad.
6. An ad where the specific merchandise cannot be illustrated.

## TYPE AND THE NEWSPAPER

While it is true that there are thousands of type faces to choose from, the number of type faces available to department store advertisers who have their ads set up by the papers are limited in number. No one paper, not even the largest metropolitan paper, can have all type faces. This isn't even possible with a typographic house whose specialty is setting advertising typography.

It is advisable, therefore, to find out what type faces and what sizes are available at your newspaper before creating a type style for your store advertising. Some papers distribute charts or books to their advertisers which show all the type faces and sizes available for advertising (pages 192-193). It is the policy of most papers not to make available to advertisers the type the paper uses for its news and editorial matter. This is good, for there should be a difference in look between advertising and editorial matter.

*If the paper doesn't have it.* While most papers have an adequate type assortment for most ads, occasions do arise when it becomes necessary to send an ad or a campaign out to be "hand set." "Hand set" is a trade phrase meaning to send the ad to a typographic house which specializes in advertising typography. This obviously costs money (most newspapers do not charge for initial typographic services). There should always be a good reason for sending an ad out to be set at a typographer's. Here are some:

1. Type faces or sizes not available at the newspaper.
2. Special handling because of a complex typographic problem.
3. Special handling because of a shorter than normal time table.
4. An advance on normal release time of a very

special ad that requires approval from more than the normal number of store executives.
5. An ad that is going to be released simultaneously to many newspapers.
6. A policy ad which should be private and not seen by many people during its advertising development.
7. Special handling for esthetic purposes only ... an expert typographer who can "baby" an ad through to its completion (which isn't always possible at the newspaper).

*Special effects.* Even with all the type faces available there are still times when a special effect cannot be achieved with type available at the newspaper or special faces at the typographic shop. The choice then is to use hand lettering or available mechanical devices.

*Hand lettering.* Unless the artist who does the lettering is very good, don't use hand lettering. Bad hand lettering is always worse than type, even type that is not just right. On the other hand, good hand lettering can enhance the ad and may give it just the touch you're looking for.

*Special type.* When you have a special typographic need, one of the new special typographic services can be performed by firms like Photo-Lettering. They have an infinite variety of special type faces, and can produce variations of type sizes, type heights, widths, perspectives, turns and twists to fit any layout space. Their service differs from a typographic house—which completes the entire ad—in that these companies specialize in pieces and parts of the ad that require special handling. (see page 194)

## HOW TO INDICATE TYPE IN A LAYOUT

This is a simple case of give and you shall receive. If the type in a layout is carefully and honestly indicated then the type proof from the paper will be as planned. Sloppy or careless indications can be interpreted at the paper in many ways, and not necessarily the one you were thinking of.

Faking or compressing type in a headline will result in either a smaller size type than expected, or a longer line than planned. (see page 195)

It may take a little more effort to be accurate, but it will save a lot of time, money and irritation in the end.

Be as precise as you can, when indicating type in a layout.

*How precise is precise?* Type characters are like people—it's a fascinating similarity. Type faces have personality. Some are short, some tall, some fat, some meek, some animated, some flowery and some just sit.

If you were asked to make a sketch of a fat person, everyone who looks at it would recognize it as a fat person. Give a name to that person, like John S., and from that point on, if you were asked to draw John S. you would draw a fat person. Now let's use the name Ultra Bodoni. Ultra Bodoni is a fat type face, it looks like this (**B**). If you want Ultra Bodoni in your ad, indicate the characteristic on the layout, and you'll get it.

People come in various sizes, so does type. The sizes, however, are far different.

## THE ARITHMETIC OF TYPE

The unit of measure for type is the American point system. There are 72 points to the inch.

Most types come in a graduation of sizes from 6 points to 72 points, some up to 120 points (the more popular the type, the more apt it is to come in all sizes).

Type sizes graduate upwards from 6 points to 16 points in these sizes:

6-7-8-9-10-11-12-14-16

From 16 points they graduate upwards by 6 points:

18-24-30-36-42-48

From 48 points they graduate upwards by 12 points (a pica): 60-72-84-96-108-120

Type sizes from 18 points to 120 points are generally considered and called display type. Type sizes below 18 point are generally called body type.

*Display type* should be indicated on a layout by lettering the size, the character, and the weight of the type (see page 195). In order to indicate the type properly, the designer should obviously be familiar with both the type face and the type family. He should know that some families of type are limited in variety and scope, others almost unlimited.

Some type families include a great number of sizes, weights and widths. Some include both Roman and italics. Some come only in capitals, others in capitals and lower case letters. Some have decorative or swash initials or exaggerated ascending and descending letters. All this information is available to the advertising designer from type specimen sheets, type books, the newspaper or the typographer.

*Body type,* 14 points or smaller, is usually indicated in a layout by ruled or hand-drawn lines. Each line should represent the width and, as closely as possible, the color of the type the designer is planning to use. Since this is body text, it is presumed that there will be more than one line of copy. Therefore, the space between the lines is called "leading." Leading can make a big difference in the way a block of copy looks and reads and should be carefully considered for design and legibility. Too much leading will make a copy block look anemic, too little will make it hard to read. Mathematical formulas have been worked out and are often useful to determine the proper leading for a given size type in a given width, but visual examples are far better. Most type books show blocks of copy in various sizes with various amounts of leading.

When the typed text calls for emphasis within the block of copy, this, too, should be indicated on the layout. Typographic variety or emphasis can be achieved by **bolder type face**, CAPS, *italics,* or underscoring.

Since body text is usually indicated on a layout by drawn rules, italics can be designated either by a line of simulated script writing or the actual lettering of the type. (This is impractical when the type is smaller than 14 point. Italics should therefore be marked on the original manuscript and written in on the side of the layout as an explanation.)

Bold face type and underscoring are simpler to show on the layout. A heavier rule indicates bold face and the underscore should be indicated by a line under the type.

One of the more complex typographic problems in department store advertising is the merchandise listing. It's complex because the copy lines cannot always be even, which results in ragged lines, and because it usually contains two or more type faces, type weights, or sizes. When the layout man indicates the listing he can make it look good because he idealizes the design. Rarely does the typographic result come out this way unless the copy has been truthfully and accurately accounted for in the space allotted. It is the layout man's responsibility to design the listing so it not only looks good on the layout, but is an honest representation of the amount of copy necessary.

## 30 DIFFERENT OPERATIONS 30

It is not the intention of this chapter to teach you to be a typographic expert, any more than the chapter on art can teach you to draw. Its purpose, rather, is to help you understand a little more clearly the importance of type and its relationship to other elements in the ad. Many points have been mentioned, some developed in detail, others just highlighted and requiring further study.

Aside from the major consideration "Type is to read," it must be remembered that before it can be read, type is set by a compositor. Again we quote from Mr. Varian, who was previously mentioned in this chapter: "You must remember that the ordinary ad going to a newspaper to be set must go through about thirty different operations in the composing room alone...

*...if everyone participating in the construction of an ad—copywriter, artist, layout man, and typographer —would first of all try to produce his or her portion of that ad as neatly and understandably as possible... the results would probably make everyone happier."*

# This is a family of type: Bodoni

This is BAUER BODONI

*This is BAUER BODONI Italic*

**This is BAUER BODONI Bold**

***This is BAUER BODONI Bold Italic***

# BAU

(THIS IS BAUER BODONI TITLE)

This is BODONI Book

*This is BODONI Book Italic*

This is BODONI

*This is BODONI Italic*

**This is BODONI Bold**

***This is BODONI Bold Italic***

**This is BODONI Bold Condensed**

## Bodoni Open

**This is Ultra BODONI**

***This is Ultra BODONI Italic***

**This is Ultra BODONI Ex. Cond.**

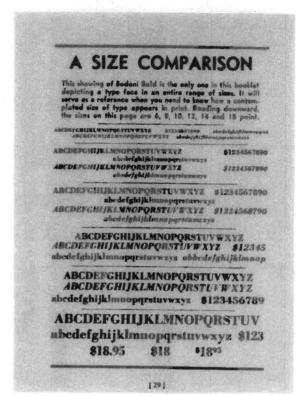

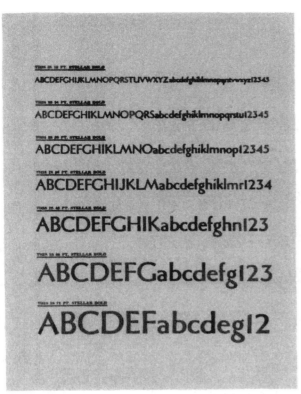

MANCHESTER EVENING HERALD: a 14 page assortment of type faces in a good range of sizes.

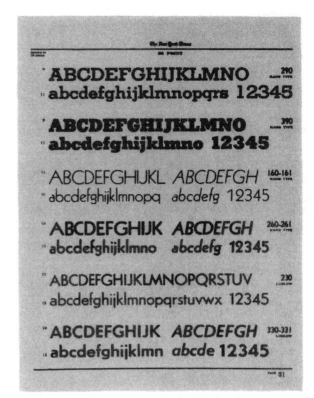

THE NEW YORK TIMES: Page 31 of a 66 page type book showing a great variety of type faces and sizes.

PLAINFIELD COURIER NEWS (N.J.): This book shows the type faces available and the number of characters that will fit in a given size and width.

THE PROVIDENCE JOURNAL AND EVENING BULLETIN (R.I.): Page 15 of a 24 page book. A comprehensive selection of type. Note the complete Cairo "family."

*The Vanishing Back*

A Madagascar Alligator Suit Shoe at one hundred and forty five dollars. but entirely hand-made in Paris Delman-Dior Salon. as this was only available custom-made gray, toast, navy, brown or black,

An example of hand lettering that creates a "spirit" which the advertising designer felt couldn't be achieved with type. Drawn by Andrew Szoerke, a master calligrapher.

**ROMANTIQUE No. 4**

## THE LAZY DOG 56

An "Odd" type face, used with discretion, can enhance an ad. From "A Showing of Quaint American Faces..." by Master Typo Co., Inc., New York.

*A touch of Palazzo is a touch of Spring*

Brush stroke lettering can add spice to an ad, but like spice, a little goes a long way. The example shown here was drawn by Eric Mulvany.

*Murray Hill Contour Shaded*

2919e **ADVERTISING follows popular trend tor**

2919c **ADVERTISING follows popular trend tor**

2919n 15° *ADVERTISING follows popular trend tor*

Custom lettering effects can be achieved by photo-lettering to solve specific typographic layout problems. Example from "Alphabet Thesaurus ..." Photo-Lettering, Inc., New York.

Ultra Bodoni type *should be indicated like this*
**Ultra Bodoni type** *should be indicated like this*

---

**Franklin Gothic, wide, condensed and extra condensed**
**Franklin Gothic, wide,** condensed and extra condensed

---

Caslon Roman *and Italic indicated like this*
Caslon Roman *and Italic indicated like this*

---

Stymie Light, Medium, **Bold and Stymie Black**
Stymie Light, Medium, **Bold and Stymie Black**

---

Bodoni Regular Roman *and Bodoni Regular Italic*
Bodoni Regular Roman *and Bodoni Regular Italic*

---

Futura Medium, identical with Spartan & Airport
Futura Medium, identical with Spartan & Airport

This is how type is indicated on a layout and how
it appears when it is actually set. The more accurate
the indication, the closer the ad will be to the layout.

Here are seventeen pages from a thirty-six page section of a daily New York newspaper. Every page except three has major space advertising. Every page is after the same consumer attention as well as the consumer dollar. With competition of this kind how can you get your ad seen and read? Read Chapter Nine.

# GRAPHIC DRAMA

*"It starts to return your investment"*

## "BARGAIN: $54,284.90 . . .

*"If an atypical consumer reading a New York newspaper the other day had bought one of everything advertised, every product and every service, the total would come to $54,284.90.*

*"He would be the owner, in return for this expenditure, of a suit, a pair of shoes, a necktie, a martini (89 cents), a 1958 Chevrolet, a jar of instant coffee, a tourist flight to Hawaii, a house, a stole ($500), a prospector's guide to Alaska, a stock option ($350), and several dozen other items.*

*"Sales Management does the figuring . . . by way of pointing up 'the tug of war that goes on daily in the minds of Mr. and Mrs. American Consumer on the way they spend their money'."*

New York Times, Wednesday, August 31, 1960
Advertising column: William M. Freeman

## IF THEY CAN'T SEE IT . . . THEY CAN'T READ IT

From page one on to the last page of Chapter 8, we have maintained one point of view based on the title "How to design effective store advertising." We related the word effective to merchandise, schedules, people, communication, layout, art, copy and typography.

These are the segments that make up the total ad. Sooner or later (and mostly sooner) the total ad has to leave the store to complete its mission and appear competitively with other ads in the newspaper. It's at this point that many ads fail.

Why do they fail?

How do you eliminate part of the risk?

Let's consider these two questions and their answers in the light of the following observations:

1. Newspaper space is probably the most valuable "real-estate" a store owns, second only to its valuable store property. *Don't waste it.*

2. Stores go to great lengths to maintain their competitive position in price, quality, resources, services and physical appearance. *Ads should reflect this—and be equally competitive.*

3. Stores constantly try to offer the right merchandise at the right price at the right time. *Ads, too, should be right—for the time, the place, the consumer.*

In spite of this great competitive urge, differences tend to neutralize themselves and become subtle. This is as true in merchandise and services as it is in advertising.

Most stores see their ads as complete entities in their own advertising department, and seldom in competitive relationship to other advertising in the newspaper.

Oh, sure, they look at the other department stores' advertising to see what the competition is doing by way of merchandising and prices.

BUT DO THEY RELATE THEIR ADVERTISING COMPETITIVELY TO ALL OTHER ADVERTISING IN THE PAPER?

Every ad in a newspaper is after the same consumer dollar the same day.

Every ad is in competition visually with every other ad in the newspaper.

While it is known that women "shop" the newspapers for department store news, exciting and dramatic competitive advertising (other than the department stores') can distract the reader, and, subtract the consumer's dollar.

It isn't enough to be satisfied that your ad tells your story—*it must tell it in a way that gets it seen—so that it can't be missed.*

This does not mean that every ad must be a full page (although big space makes it easier). It does, however, mean that whatever the size it must be seen . . . quickly.

How quickly? Consider this . . .

All of us in retailing are more and more conscious of TV advertising. We argue that TV advertising is ephemeral and fleeting. It comes and goes and there's no recall . . . no second look.

But newspaper advertising we say is the opposite. It's solid. You can hold it in your hand. You can read it again and again. It has total recall. In the newspapers you can have hundreds of words and many illustrations to help sell. In the newspaper the reader has all the time in the world. That's the way we argue ... But is it so?

To go back to TV for a moment. We know that among the many ways to get our message across on television is the one minute commercial, another is the 8 to 10 second I. D. (station identification). Sixty seconds is a reasonable time in which to get a message across, even if you have to repeat the salient facts three times. Eight seconds (the I. D.) is a very short time (see how much you can say effectively in eight seconds).

Eight seconds is the total time to get your selling message across in an I. D. Eight seconds is ephemeral.

But even though the newspaper is not ephemeral, not fleeting ... you often have less than eight seconds.

*The casual reader (a customer, too) takes between 3 and 4 seconds to turn the page of a standard size paper.* This has been checked and proven with a stop watch time and again.

Four seconds and all your meetings, your planning, your copy, art work, your dollars are gone ... *all because you haven't stopped the reader.*

Everything that was supposed to get into the ad to tell your complete story got into it, including the manufacturer's name, the copy, the front as well as the back view of the dress and the cute sailboat in the background. (It suggests that the dress is great to wear at the sea-shore). It's all in the ad, but in such a way that it falls into the gray area of oblivion. What's missing? The stopping power, the positive quality that says ... look! read!

What's missing? *GRAPHIC DRAMA!*

Graphic drama is the competitive factor required to get your ad seen in the newspaper.

Graphic drama will buy you the reading time that you're paying for. Graphic drama says ... Stop! Look! Read!

## HOW DO YOU ACHIEVE GRAPHIC DRAMA?

A great many of the formulas discussed in this book were basic. When these are understood and assimilated, the ad designer starts on his search for new excitement. In his search he may break every rule of formalized design.

Couple this urge with a good merchandising sense and a great deal of good taste and he's on his way to producing ads with graphic drama. He knows that he's got to make his ads lighter or darker than competition's, or bigger or smaller in the ad space;

he knows that it's got to be different, pleasantly different.

Pleasantly different quickly eliminates the upside down ad and the buck-eye black ads which may startle but may also irritate the reader. These have graphic drama too, but also graphic trauma.

There are many ways to create graphic drama of the right kind. Just consider these:

### 1
ADS THAT CONTAIN DELIBERATE REPETITION OF GRAPHIC ELEMENTS.

### 2
ADS WITH ART OR TYPE OF UNUSUAL SCALE.

### 3
ADS THAT CONTAIN ELEMENTS OF SURPRISE.

### 4
ADS THAT ARE DESIGNED WITH POSITIVE AND UNUSUAL SHAPES.

### 5
ADS THAT CONTAIN UNUSUAL ART TREATMENTS.

### 6
ADS WITH AN UNUSUAL TYPOGRAPHIC MESSAGE.

### 7
ADS THAT HAVE GREAT COLOR OR TEXTURE CONTRAST.

### 8
ADS THAT ARE CONTEMPORARY (AS FRESH AS TODAY'S NEWSPAPER).

### 9
ADS WITH A NON-FAMILIAR FORMAT.

### 10
ADS WITH A DYNAMIC FOCAL POINT.

**GRAPHIC DRAMA WILL GET THE AD SEEN AND READ. AND UNTIL THE AD IS SEEN AND READ, THE MERCHANDISE CANNOT BE SOLD.**

Printed by the Lehigh Printing Co.